Que® Quick Reference Series

Windows 3® Quick Reference

Timothy S. Stanley

Que® Corporation
Carmel, Indiana

Windows 3 Quick Reference.

Copyright ©1990 by Que Corporation.

Library of Congress Catalog Number: 90-62079

ISBN 0-88022-631-5

93   92   91   4   3

Interpretation of the printing code: the rightmost double-digit number is the year of the book's printing; the rightmost single-digit number is the number of the book's printing. For example, a printing code of 90-4 shows that the fourth printing of the book occurred in 1990.

This book is based on Windows Version 3.

Que Quick Reference Series

The *Que Quick Reference Series* is a portable resource of essential microcomputer knowledge. Whether you are a new or experienced user, you can rely on the high-quality information contained in these convenient guides.

Drawing on the experience of many of Que's best-selling authors, the *Que Quick Reference Series* helps you easily access important program information.

Now it's easy to look up often-used commands and functions for 1-2-3, dBASE IV, WordPerfect 5, Microsoft Word 5, and MS-DOS, as well as programming information for C, Turbo Pascal, and QuickBASIC 4.

Use the *Que Quick Reference Series* as a compact alternative to confusing and complicated traditional documentation.

The *Que Quick Reference Series* includes these titles:

1-2-3 Quick Reference
1-2-3 Release 2.2 Quick Reference
1-2-3 Release 3 Quick Reference
Assembly Language Quick Reference
AutoCAD Quick Reference
C Quick Reference
dBASE IV Quick Reference
DOS and BIOS Functions Quick Reference
Excel Quick Reference
Hard Disk Quick Reference
Harvard Graphics Quick Reference
MS-DOS Quick Reference
Microsoft Word 5 Quick Reference
Norton Utilities Quick Reference
PC Tools Quick Reference
Q&A Quick Reference
QuickBASIC Quick Reference
Turbo Pascal Quick Reference
WordPerfect Quick Reference
WordPerfect 5.1 Quick Reference

Publishing Director
  Lloyd J. Short

Series Product Director
  Karen A. Bluestein

Senior Production Editor
  Cheryl S. Robinson

Technical Editor
  Jim Karney

Proofreader
  Betty Kish

Indexer
  Hilary Adams

Table of Contents

Introduction

Windows 3 Quick Reference not only includes the quick
reference information you need to manage applications,
but reviews the various commands, options, and
applications available with Windows 3. You learn to
work with associated programs such as Cardfile, File
Manager, and Notepad, and the other accessories that
accompany Windows.

Because it is a quick reference, this book is not intended
to replace the extensive documentation included with
Windows 3. For further information, supplement this
book with Que's *Using Windows,* 2nd Edition.

This Quick Reference highlights the most frequently
used information and reference material required to
work quickly and efficiently with Windows. For
example, the documentation includes pages of
information on how to use the File Manager. *Windows 3
Quick Reference* does not repeat that extensive
documentation. Instead, this book provides step-by-step
instructions on how to perform many of the tasks
involved in using the File Manager.

This book is divided into sections by tasks. One task, for
example, is called "Searching for Text". This section
provides the step-by-step instructions needed to search
for text using the Notepad.

Now you can put essential information at your fingertips
with *Windows 3 Quick Reference*—and the entire Que
Quick Reference series.

Windows Applications

Windows 3.0 is a multitasking operating environment for MS-DOS. It is called an "environment" because programs are designed to work in, and take advantage of Windows. Windows manages the applications that are designed for it, giving all programs a similar, consistent look and feel, and enables you to operate more than one program at a time. Although you may have Windows so that you can use powerful programs such as Excel, Word for Windows, and PageMaker, you cannot overlook the following accessories that accompany Windows:

Accessory	*Description*
Notepad	Simple text editor used to record reminder notes, or to create and modify ASCII files, such as Batch files.
Recorder	Creates macros of repetitious keystrokes and mouse movements.
Cardfile	Card-type database (such as a Rolodex).
Calendar	Appointment scheduler with alarm.
Calculator	Desktop calculator with scientific and financial functions.
Clock	An on-screen analog or digital clock.
PIF Editor	Creates Program Information Files to enable DOS applications to run in the Windows environment.
File Manager	A shell to manage directories and files.

Clipboard	Holds text or graphics that you want transferred between programs
Control Panel	Customizes Windows.
Print Manager	Enables Windows to manage and spool print jobs.
Window Setup	Sets up Windows and add applications, creating PIFs automatically.

Windows 3 also contains the following accessories that are not covered in this book:

Accessory	*Description*
Paintbrush	A bit-map drawing program that supports colors.
Terminal	A communications program.
Write	A simple word processor.

Hints for Using This Book

Because Windows 3 consists of many different accessories, this Quick Reference includes a subhead under each boxed header referring you to a specific Windows 3 area. The subhead tells you which program to run to achieve the desired result.

For example, you see the words "File Manager" under the heading "Selecting Files." This subhead tells you that the commands you need to execute are located in the File Manager.

Conventions used in this book

As you use this book, you need to know a few terms and methods of carrying out actions. Most instruction provide two ways to access the menu; using the keyboard and using the mouse.

Press **Alt-O**.

To use the keyboard, press **Alt-O**. That means to press and hold **Alt**, press **O**, and then release both keys. You press the keys associated with the boldfaced blue letters. The word that contains the boldfaced character will be the name of a menu, a menu item, or an option that you select. Note that the boldfaced letter appears underlined on the Windows screen.

Click the **Options** menu with the left mouse button.

If you have a mouse, you move the mouse until the on-screen arrow is on the menu item. To click, means to press and release the left button on the mouse. When you double-click the mouse button, you rapidly press and release the left mouse button twice.

Terms to Remember

A *dialog box* is a box that appears to give you a message, or to enable you to select other options. Normally, the dialog box has a Title Bar, telling you the purpose of the box.

When you *choose* an item, you cause the item to activate. Sometimes you can choose an item, such as a menu or menu option with the mouse by just clicking the mouse button. Other times, as with icons, you must double-click the mouse button in order to choose the item.

Selecting an item means to prepare the item to be acted on. This usually entails highlighting the item. For example, before you copy a file, you select the file; that is, before you act on the file by copying it, you must select it, or highlight it.

The Windows Desktop

Notice the sample Desktop shown in the figure. Each part of the Desktop is labeled with a number. Consult the list that follows the figure for a description of the numbered item.

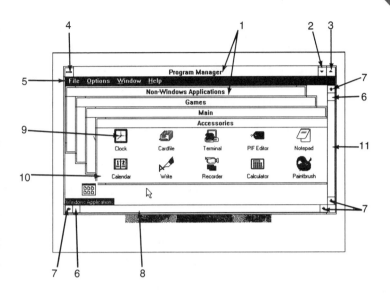

The following is a list of elements that make up the Desktop:

Element	*Description*
1 Title bar	Tells you the name of the program and data file if applicable, or the name of the dialog box.
2 Minimize button	Reduces the size of the window.
3 Maximize button	Expands the open window.
4 Control menu	Offers the options Restore, Move, Size, Minimize, Maximize, Close, and Switch To.

5 Menu bar   Displays the menu items used
                      to control the application.

6 Scroll box   Displays your file position.
                      Can be "dragged" to move
                      your position in the file.

7 Scroll arrows   Controls the scroll box.

8 Scroll bar   Combines the action of the
                      scroll arrows and scroll box.

9 Icon   A small picture that appears if
                      an application is minimized or
                      yet to be activated.

10 Window   The entire entity made up of at
                      least a Control menu, Title bar,
                      and borders.

11 Window border The outside frame of the
                      window.

COMMAND REFERENCE

Following is an alphabetical listing of Windows
commands and the procedures required to achieve
specific results.

386 Enhanced Options

Control Panel

Purpose

Enables Windows to better manage running a Windows
application (such as Excel) with a non-Windows
application (such as WordPerfect). The 386 Enhanced
options manage the use of parallel and serial ports by
warning you if two applications try to use the same port.

These options also manage how much computer time is allotted to each program. Windows slices time, and gives each application a *timeslice*. You may customize each timeslice with 386 Enhanced options.

Procedures

To set 386 Enhanced options

1. Start the Control Panel.

2. Press the arrow keys to select the 386 Enhanced icon and then press **Enter**.

   or

   Point to the icon with the mouse and double-click the left mouse button.

3. Select **D**evice Contention by pressing **Alt-D,** or by pointing to the first device in the **D**evice Contention box and pressing the left mouse button.

4. Select the device to set up.

   For example, select COM1.

5. Select either **A**lways Warn, **N**ever Warn, or **I**dle (in sec.) by pressing **Alt-A**, **Alt-N**, or **Alt-I**, or by pointing to one of the options and pressing the left mouse button. The meaning of the options are as follows:

Option	*Function*
Always Warn	Displays a message when a program tries to access a port that is being used. You choose the application that gets access to the port. In most instances, choose this option.
Never Warn	Enables any application to use any port at any time without warning. Choosing this option may cause problems. For example, if two applications send information to the printer,

your printout may contain information from both applications. In most instances, do not select this option.

Idle (in sec.)   Allows an application access to a port only if the port has not been used for a specified number of seconds. If you select this option, you must specify the number of seconds that a port should set idle.

6. Repeat steps 3 through 5 for additional ports.

7. Select Windows in Foreground. Type a number from 1 to 10,000. The default setting is 100.

   This option specifies how much computer time a Windows application should get when it is in the foreground, and a non-Windows application is running in the background. The larger the number, the more time that is allotted.

8. Select Windows in Background. Type a number from 1 to 10,000. The default setting is 50.

   This option specifies how much computer time a Windows application is given when it is running in the background, and a non-Windows application is running in the foreground. The larger the number, the more time that is allotted.

9. Select Exclusive in Foreground if you want a Windows application to get all the computer time when it is in the foreground, even though a non-Windows application is running in the background. If you select this option, the foreground Windows application will get 100 percent of the computer time, while the non-Windows application will halt. When the non-Windows application is made the foreground application again, it will operate again as normal.

10. Select Minimum Timeslice (in msec). Enter the number of milliseconds (thousandths of a second) that an application gets when it receives a timeslice.

11. To save the changes, press **Enter** or click **OK** with
the left mouse button.

Notes

Device contention manages what takes place when a
non-Windows application tries to use a port that is
managed by Windows.

These options also manage how much computer time is
allotted to each program. Windows slices time, and
gives each application a *timeslice*. Each DOS application
is given one timeslice. All Windows applications that
run concurrently must share a timeslice. You can
customize each timeslice with 386 Enhanced options.
The manner in which you allot the timeslices can affect
how applications operate during multitasking.

386 Enhanced Mode

PIF Editor

Purpose

Creates a Program Information File (PIF) that contains
information that Windows must know in order to
allocate computer resources for the program.

Procedures

To select the 386 Enhanced mode

1. Start the PIF Editor accessory.

2. Select the **M**ode menu.

   A check mark appears next to the currently selected
   mode.

3. If the check mark does not appear next to 386
   Enhanced, then select **3**86 Enhanced.

**To enter information for the 386 Enhanced Mode (using
Lotus 1-2-3 Release 2.2 as an example)**

1. Select **P**rogram Filename.

Enter the entire file name used to start the program within the box. Include the path, root name, and extension. In this example, type

C:\123\LOTUS.COM.

2. Select Window Title.

Enter the name that appears at the top of the window. For example, type **Lotus Access System**.

3. Select **O**ptional Parameters. These parameters are used when the program starts, such as switches.

Lotus 1-2-3 allows you to supply a different configuration, called a SET file. For example, you can type **COLOR.SET**, if it is the name of a valid configuration file.

4. Select **S**tart-up Directory.

Enter the directory name that the program will use. Some programs store their data in the current directory. In this example, type **C:\123**.

5. Enter the memory required to run the program in the KB **R**equired field. For example, if the minimum memory required to run the program is 256K, then type **256**.

6. Enter the memory desired to run the program in the KB **D**esired field. For example, if the memory desired to run the program is 640K, then type **640**.

8. Select how the program should be displayed. Under Display Usage, select F**u**ll Screen if the program should use the entire screen, or **W**indowed if the program can run in a window, sharing the screen with other applications.

9. Specify Execution. Select **B**ackground if the program should continue operating when it is not the foreground program. If you do not select **B**ackground, the program will halt when it is switched from the foreground. Select **E**xclusive if the program should have full access to the computer when it is in the foreground. All other programs will halt.

10. Select **C**lose Window on Exit if you want the window to close when you quit the program.

To see the 386 Enhanced mode's Advanced options

1. From the main PIF Editor window, select Advanced.

2. Enter a number from 1 to 10,000 for the Background Priority. The default number is 50.

3. Enter a number from 1 to 10,000 for the Foreground Priority. The default number is 100.

4. Selecting Detect Idle Time enables Windows to see whether the current program is in a waiting condition, such as waiting for keyboard input. If the program is waiting, more computer time will be allocated to a background task.

5. Enter the minimum amount of EMS Memory (expanded memory) that the application requires in the KB Required field. Enter an exact number or 0 if no EMS memory is needed.

   If the application requires 350K of EMS memory, for example, then type 350.

6. Enter the maximum amount of EMS Memory the application may use in the KB Limit field. Enter -1 if the application may use as much expanded memory as is needed, 0 if the application is not to access expanded memory, or an exact number which is equal to or greater than the number that you entered for KB Required.

   If 512K is the most expanded memory to which the application can gain access, then enter 512 in the KB Limit field.

7. Select Locked if the application using EMS memory should not be swapped to disk. The application then will be locked into memory.

8. Enter the minimum amount of XMS Memory (extended memory) that the application requires. In the KB Required field, enter 0 if no XMS memory is needed or an exact number.

   If the application requires 350K of XMS memory, then type 350.

9. Enter the maximum amount of XMS Memory the application may use in the KB Limit field. Enter -1 if the application may use as much extended memory as is needed, 0 if the application is not to access extended memory, or an exact number which is equal to or greater than the number that you entered in the KB Required field.

    If 512K is the most extended memory to which the application can gain access, then type 512.

10. Select LocKed to keep the application in memory only, which does not allow the application to be swapped to disk.

11. Select the Video Memory display option. Select Text if the application only displays text. Choose Low Graphics or High Graphics if the application displays graphics. Text requires less memory than High Graphics. Select between Text, Low Graphics, or High Graphics using the arrow keys or by clicking the option with the left mouse button.

12. Select the Monitor PorTs display option. Select Text, Low Graphics, or High Graphics, depending on how the software is installed. Select between Text, Low Graphics, or High Graphics by using the arrow keys and space bar, or by clicking the option with the left mouse button.

13. Select Emulate Text mode to make a text-only application refresh the screen quicker.

    If the screen becomes garbled while Emulate Text Mode is selected, then deselect Emulate Text Mode.

14. Select Retain Video Memory to save the screen when you switch from the program.

    When you select this option, the memory is set aside, and not given back, even if you change video modes. The memory set aside is freed when you close the application.

15. Select Allow Fast Paste if the application allows text to be pasted to it.

16. Select Allow Close When Active to designate a drastic way to quit a non-Windows application.

Note that closing an application other than with the
normal procedure can cause data to be damaged or
lost.

17. Select Reserve Shortcut Keys to enable the program
    to use the key combinations Alt+Tab, Alt+Esc,
    Ctrl+Esc, PrtSc, or Alt+PrtSc.

    Select each key combination using the arrow keys
    and the space bar, or by clicking the option you
    want with the left mouse button.

    Windows then ignores each key combination that
    you select while running that program.

18. Select Application Shortcut Key to make the
    application the current application using a key
    combination.

19. To quit making changes to Advanced Options,
    press **Enter** or click **OK** with the left mouse button.

    To abort the Advanced Options, press **Esc** or click
    Cancel.

To save the PIF

1. Select the File menu.

2. Select Save As.

3. Select FileName and type the name of the PIF,
   following the standard DOS convention of no more
   than eight characters per name.

4. Press **Enter** or click **OK** with the left mouse button
   to complete the save.

Notes

PIFs for Windows running in Standard mode differ from
PIFs for 386 Enhanced mode. A Standard mode PIF
contains information on memory requirements, type of
screen (text or graphics), and whether the program
directly communicates with a serial port. If you have a
computer based on the 80386 microprocessor and
operate in 386 Enhanced Mode, however, you can run
several DOS applications at once. To multitask
applications, Windows must have more information
about each application than it requires to run just a
single DOS application.

Selecting 386 Enhanced Mode enables you to specify whether the application can run in a window or must occupy the entire screen. You also must specify whether the application can operate in background. If you specify that the application can run in background, you must allot how much computer time is given to the background application.

Adding Appointments

Calendar

Purpose

Records appointments that you need to remember for an entire day.

Procedures

To add an appointment

1. Start the Calendar accessory.

2. Select the appointment day by pressing **Ctrl-PgUp** and **Ctrl-PgDn** or by clicking the right and left arrows on the status bar.

3. Select the appointment time by pressing the **up-** and **down-arrow** keys or by clicking the correct time.

4. Type the note for the appointment.

5. Set an alarm if necessary.

6. Save the calendar file.

To save the calendar file

1. Select **F**ile by pressing **Alt-F** or by clicking **F**ile.

2. Select Save **A**s.

3. Select File**N**ame and type the name of the PIF, following the standard DOS naming conventions.

4. Press **Enter** or click **OK** with the left mouse button to complete the save.

Note

The appointments may simply be reminders for you to reference, or you can set an alarm so that a bell sounds at the appointed time, when it is time, or near time for the appointment.

Adding Cards

Cardfile

Purpose

Enables you to place more information in the cardfile database.

Procedure

1. Start the Cardfile Accessory.

2. Choose the Card menu by pressing Alt-C, or by clicking Card with the left mouse button.

3. Choose Add.

4. When the Add dialog box appears, type the information for the index line of the card in the Add field.

5. Press Enter or click OK with the left mouse button.

   To abandon the procedure, choose Cancel by pressing Esc or by clicking Cancel with the left mouse button.

Notes

Adding a new card to the cardfile database is similar to adding a new page to your address book, or adding a card to your Rolodex.

When adding a card, you see an Add dialog box. In the dialog box, you type the information for quick search. Enter the same information in this line that you enter in your index line of each card. For example, if you search the cards by name, type the name that will be assigned to the new card.

Adding Notes

Notepad

Purpose

Enables you to type text in the Notepad and save the text to an ASCII file. The Notepad is basically a simple word processor and text editor with a file size limit of 50K.

Procedure

1. Start the Notepad accessory.

2. If you want to add new notes to an existing file, retrieve the file from disk using the File Open command.

3. Position the cursor at the end of the existing document by pressing the arrow keys, or move the mouse until the I-beam bar is at the end of the existing text, then click the left mouse button.

4. Type the new text. Be sure to save the document after you make changes using the File Save or File Save As commands.

Notes

Because the Notepad saves its information in standard ASCII text, you will find the Notepad to be more useful that just to type reminder notes to yourself. You also can use the notepad to modify the computer's AUTOEXEC.BAT and CONFIG.SYS files. In addition, you may also edit Windows configuration file. The Notepad also can be used as a program editor.

Adding Program Groups

Program Manager

Purpose

Enables you to keep like programs together. Use this option to create a new Program Group.

Procedure

1. Select the Program Manager.

2. Select the File menu by pressing **Alt-F** or by clicking **File** with the left mouse button.

3. From the File menu, select New.

4. From the New Program Object dialog box, select Program Group.

5. Press **Enter** or click **OK** with the left mouse button.

   The Program Group Properties dialog box appears on-screen.

6. Select the Description field, and type the name of the new group.

   For example, type **WORDPROCESSING**.

7. Select the Group File field, and type the name of the file you want to contain the new program group information.

   For example, type

   C:\WINDOWS\WORDPROC.GRP.

8. Press **Enter** or click **OK** to save the new Program Group.

Note

When you installed Windows, the following program groups may have been created: Main, Accessories,

Windows Applications, Non-Windows Applications, and Games. These groups logically separate different kinds of applications. You may decide, however, to create a program group that contains your word processing and accompanying applications. When you add a new program group, you must name the on-screen icon and designate a file name. Make sure that you do not duplicate a program group name or file name.

Adding Program Items

Program Manager

Purpose

Adds an icon to a Program Group so that you can start each program from this icon.

Procedure

1. Open the Program Manager.

2. Press **Alt-W** or click the **Window** menu with the left mouse button to open the Program Group to which you want to add the Program Item.

3. Choose the File menu by pressing **Alt-F**, or by clicking the File menu with the left mouse button.

4. Choose New by pressing **N**, or by clicking the New option with the left mouse button.

   The New Program Object appears on-screen.

5. Select Program Item by pressing **I**, or by clicking **Program Item** with the left mouse button.

6. Press **Enter** or click **OK** with the left mouse button. The Program Item Properties dialog box appears on-screen.

   To cancel the operation, press **Esc** or click **Cancel** with the left mouse button.

7. Press **Alt-D** or click the **Description** field with the left mouse button. Type the name that will appear under the icon.

Suppose, for example, that you want to add Lotus 1-2-3. You might type LOTUS 1-2-3 for the description.

8. Press Alt-C or click Command Line with the left mouse button. Type the name of the file that starts the program. You may have to include the path pointing to the file.

Suppose, for example, that you created a PIF for Lotus 1-2-3, and stored the PIF in C:\123. Type C:\123\123.PIF.

If you do not know the name of the file, choose press Alt-B or click the Browse button with the left mouse button. The Browse dialog box lists files that you can choose.

9. To change the icon, press Alt-I or click the Change Icon button with the left mouse button. The Select Icon dialog box appears on-screen.

10. Press Alt-F or click the File Name field with the left mouse button. Type PROGMAN.EXE.

11. Press Alt-N or click the View Next button with the left mouse button.

Each time you choose View Next, the icon changes. Change to the desired icon and press Enter, or click OK button with the left mouse button.

12. To finish adding the program item, choose OK by pressing Enter or by clicking OK with the left mouse button.

To cancel the operation, press Esc or click Cancel with the left mouse button.

Notes

Each program in a Program Group is displayed as an icon and called a Program Item. When you installed Windows, several Program Items were created for you. For example, the Accessories Program Group contains the following ten Program Items: Write, Paintbrush, Terminal, Notepad, Recorder, Cardfile, Calendar, Calculator, Clock, and PIF Editor.

Alarm Settings

Calendar

Purpose

Sets an audible alarm to remind you of important appointments.

Procedures

To turn on an alarm for a specific time

1. Select the alarm time by using the arrow keys to move to the correct time, or by pointing to the correct time and clicking the left mouse button.

2. Select Alarm.

3. Select Set.

To reset an alarm

1. Select the time to reset the alarm using the arrow keys or by clicking with the mouse.

2. Select Alarm.

3. Select Set.

To shut off an alarm that is ringing

1. Select the Alarm application.

2. Select OK from the message dialog box by pressing **Enter** or by clicking **OK** with the left mouse button.

Application Installation

Setup

Purpose

Searches your hard disk for programs you already installed.

To install applications that Windows Setup can look for

1. Open the Main Program Group from the Program Manager.

2. Select Windows Setup by choosing the icon with the **left-** or **right-arrow** keys and pressing **Enter**.

   or

   Double-click the **Windows Setup** icon .

3. From Windows Setup, select Options.

4. Select Set Up Applications.

5. From the Set Up Applications dialog box, select the drive you want to search or select All Drives.

6. Select OK by pressing **Enter** or clicking **OK** with the left mouse button.

7. From the list of programs under Applications found on hard disk(s), select the applications for use with Windows.

8. Select Add to specify the applications chosen or select ADd All.

9. Press **Tab** until OK is highlighted; then press **Enter**.

   or

   Click **OK** with the left mouse button.

To exit from Windows Setup

1. Select Options.

2. Select EXit.

Notes

Using this Setup option enables you to install programs to run Windows. When Setup installs applications, it creates a list of the programs that it is aware of and finds. You then select which of these applications should be set up as a Program Item, creating an icon for the program. If the program is a non-Windows program, then a PIF is created for the program.

You must manually add programs for which Windows is not aware. See 386 Enhanced Mode-PIF Editor, Standard Mode-PIF Editor, and Adding Program Items-Program Manager.

Arranging Icons

Program Manager

Purpose

Arranges icons so that you easily can read the title below each icon. When a program group window is open, icons can become in disarray so that you cannot see which applications reside in the program group. You can set up each program group window so that the icons automatically are arranged.

Procedures

To move an icon using a mouse

1. Point to the icon and press and hold the left mouse button.

2. Drag the mouse until the icon is in the desired location.

3. Release the mouse button.

To move an icon using the keyboard

1. Open the program group whose icons need moved.

2. Choose the icon you want to move using the Shift-arrow keys.

3. Press **Alt-Hyphen** to open the Control menu.`

4. Select **M**ove.

5. Press the arrow keys to move the icon.

6. Press **Enter** to complete the icon move.

To arrange all icons in a window

1. Select the window whose icons need arranged.

2. Select the **W**indow menu by pressing **Alt-W** or by pointing and clicking with the mouse.

3. Select Arrange Icons.

To set up the program manager so that all icons are arranged automatically

1. From the Program Manager, select Options.

2. Select Auto Arrange. A check mark appears next to the option after it is selected.

Notes

The arrangement of the icons depends greatly on the shape of the window. Suppose, for example, that the window is tall and skinny. The icons are arranged in columns. If the window is short and fat, however, the icons are arranged in rows. You may notice that when you arrange icons, some of the icon names overlap. You can change the spacing of icons or edit the icon names so that they do not overlap. See *Desktop Customization*.

Arranging Windows

Program Manager

Purpose

Arranges windows so that you can view more than one window at a time.

Procedures

To move a window using a mouse

1. Activate the window by pointing to it and clicking the left mouse button.

2. Point to the title bar and press and hold the left mouse button.

3. As you drag the mouse, the window moves.

4. When the window is in a desired position, release the mouse button.

To move a window using the keyboard

1. Activate the window by pressing Alt-Esc.

2. Select the Control menu by pressing **Alt-space bar**.

3. Select **M**ove.

4. Using the arrow keys, move thc window to the desired position.

5. Press **Enter** when you have the window in the desired position.

Notes

You can arrange windows so that the window you want to reference is not overlapped by other windows. You can keep windows small and place them side-by-side. Maximize the window located in the foreground, and minimize the window that is not in use. The term for this method is *tiling*. The second method keeps all the windows the same size, but stair-steps each window. The term for this method is *cascading*.

═ Associate Files ═══════════

File Manager

Purpose

Starst an application when you choose an application's data file.

Procedures

To associate a file to a program

1. Start the File Manager.

2. Using the arrow keys, select a directory by highlighting the name and pressing **Enter**.

   or

   Point to the directory and click the left mouse button.

3. Select a file by pressing the arrow keys to highlight the name, or by clicking the file name with the left mouse button.

4. Choose the **F**ile menu.

5. Choose Associate.

6. In the Associate dialog box, type the program name to which you want the file associated.

   For example, type **NOTEPAD.EXE**.

7. Press **Enter** or click **OK** with the left mouse button.

To start a program using an associated file

1. Start the File Manager.

2. Press the arrow keys to select the directory and press **Enter**.

   or

   Point to the directory and click the left mouse button.

3. Press the arrow keys to select the correct file and press **Enter**.

   or

   Point to the file and double-click the left mouse button

   If the file has been correctly associated, the associated program starts, and the file is retrieved into the program.

Notes

You can specify that when certain files are selected, their respectful applications start. For example, you can specify that files with the extension .NTE start Windows' Notepad accessory. When you select a file with an .NTE extension, Notepad starts and the file is ready for editing.

Calculator

Accessory

Purpose

Performs mathematical, financial, and scientific calculations.

Procedures

To start the Calculator accessory

1. Open the Accessories program group window from the Program Manager.

2. Choose the Calculator accessory.

To calculate values with the standard calculator using the keyboard

1. Turn on Num Lock.

2. Use the numeric keypad that corresponds to the calculator keys. The following table lists the keys to use for each function.

Key	Function
+	Addition
-	Subtraction
*	Multiplication
/	Division
%	Percentage
= or Enter	Equals
r	Reciprocal (1/x)
Esc	Clear
Del	Clear Entry
Ctrl+P	Memory Add
Ctrl+C	Memory Clear
Ctrl+R	Memory Recall
Ctrl+M	Memory Store
@	Square Root

To calculate values with the scientific calculator using the keyboard

1. Turn on Num Lock.

2. Use the numeric keypad that corresponds to the calculator keys. The following table lists the keys for each function in addition to the keys that you can use with the standard calculator.

Key	Function
o	Cosine
m	DMS
x	Exponent
F4	Gradients
h	Hyperbolic
i	Inverse (sin, cos, tan)
n	Natural Log
l	Common Logarithm
!	Factorial
p	PI
F3	Radians
s	Sine
t	Tangent
y	x^y
@	Square
#	Cube
v	Floating Point/ Exponential toggle
Ctrl+A	Average
Ins	Dat
Ctrl+D	Standard Deviation
Ctrl+S	Statistics
Ctrl+T	Sum
F8	Binary
F4	Byte
F6	Decimal
F2	4 Byte

Key	Function
F5	Hexadecimal
F7	Octal
F3	2 Byte
&	And
;	Integer
<	Left Shift
%	Modulus
~	Not
|	Or
^	Xor

To calculate values with the standard or scientific calculator using the mouse

Point to the desired calculator button and click the left mouse button.

To use the scientific calculator

1. Choose the View menu.

2. Choose Scientific.

To use the standard calculator

1. Choose the View menu.

2. Choose STandard.

Notes

The calculator accessory enables you to perform normal mathematic calculations. The calculator also performs many powerful functions. You can perform financial calculations as well as scientific calculations. You can copy the results of a calculation and paste the result in another application.

Changing Colors

Control Panel

Purpose

Enables you to use many different colors so that you customize the screen colors.

Procedures

To begin selecting colors

1. From the Program Manager, open the Main program group.

2. Start the Control Panel.

3. Choose the Settings menu.

4. Choose Color.

To select a new color scheme

1. Select Color Schemes by pressing S, or clicking the drop-list arrow.

2. Press the **up-** and **down-arrow** keys and press **Enter**, or point to the correct scheme and click the left mouse button.

   - Windows default
   - Arizona
   - Bordeaux
   - Designer
   - Florescent
   - Monochrome
   - Ocean
   - Patchwork
   - Rugby
   - Pastel
   - Wing tips

To change the color of an element of the screen

1. Choose Color Palette by pressing **P**, or clicking the **Color Palette** button with the mouse.

2. Choose Screen Element by pressing **E**, or clicking the drop-list arrow.

3. Press the **up-** and **down-arrow** keys to select the correct screen element and then press **Enter**.

   or

   Point to the correct element and click the left mouse button.

   The screen elements you can choose are as follows:

   - Desktop
   - Application workspace
   - Window background
   - Window text
   - Menu bar
   - Menu text
   - Active title bar
   - Inactive title bar
   - Title bar text
   - Active border
   - Inactive border
   - Window frame
   - Scroll bars

   Note: If you are using a mouse, you may point to the screen element on the representation of the screen and click the left mouse button rather than selecting the screen element from the list.

4. Choose Basic Colors by pressing **B**, or by pointing to one of the colors and clicking the left mouse button.

5. Press the **up-** and **down-arrow** keys to choose the correct color for the element and then press the **space bar**.

   or

Point to the correct color and click the left mouse button.

To define custom colors

1. Choose Custom Colors by pressing C, or clicking a custom color box.

2. Choose Define Custom Colors.

3. From the Custom Color Selector dialog box, choose the Hue, Sat, Lum, Red, Green or Blue. These settings enable you to mix the three colors and set the brightness and richness of the overall color.

4. Type the value of the new. If you are using a mouse, click the scroll boxes to change the values.

   Note that you can point to a position in the color box to select a custom color, rather than typing values for the Hue, Sat, Lum, Red, Green or Blue.

5. To save the custom color and continue creating new colors, choose Add Color by pressing A, or clicking the Add Color button with the mouse.

   To save the custom color and stop creating custom colors, choose Close by pressing C, or clicking on the Close button with the mouse.

To save a custom color scheme

1. Select the correct colors for each screen element as described in the preceding instructions.

2. Choose SAve Scheme by pressing A or clicking the Save Scheme button.

3. Type the name of the new color scheme in the Save Scheme dialog box.

4. Press Enter or click OK.

To quit making color changes

1. Choose Cancel to abandon the changes you made to the colors. Press Tab until the Cancel button is selected; then press Enter.

   or

   Click the Cancel button.

2. Press **Tab** until the OK button is selected; then press **Enter**.

or

Click the **OK** button.

Notes

Change the colors so that the screen is pleasing to your eyes. Choose colors to make each Window easy to use at a glance. For example, you should see at a glance which window is active, what the title of the active window is, and the contents of each visible window.

You can pick from the standard colors in the Windows palette, or custom-create your own color variations. You can save a set of colors so that you can change from set to set of colors.

As you set colors, watch the sample screen in the Color dialog box to ensure the mixture of colors is to your liking. Remember that some colors change appearance when other colors are added around them.

Changing the Directory View

File Manager

Purpose

Enables you to view file names only or file names and file statistics.

Procedures

To view only file names in a directory

1. Open a directory (see *View a Directory*).

2. Choose the View menu.

3. Choose Name.

To view the file name, size, date, time, and attributes in a directory

1. Open a directory (see *View a Directory*).

2. Choose the View menu.

3. Choose File Details.

To customize the file attributes you can view

1. Open a directory (see *View a Directory*).

2. Choose the View menu.

3. Choose Other.

4. From the View Other dialog box, press **Tab** to select Size, Last Modification Date, Last Modification Time, File Flags, or Set System Defaults. Press the **space bar** to select or deselect each option.

   If you have a mouse, point to each option and click the left mouse button.

5. Select OK to keep the changes to the view or Cancel to abandon the changes. To choose each button, press **Tab** until the button is selected, and then press **Enter**.

   or

   Point to the button with the mouse and press the left mouse button.

To view all the files in a directory sorted by name

1. Open a directory (see *View a Directory*).

2. Choose the View menu.

3. Choose By Name.

To view all the files in a directory sorted by type

1. Open a directory (see *View a Directory*).

2. Choose the View menu.

3. Choose By Type.

To sort and view all the files in a directory

1. Open a directory (see *View a Directory*).

2. Choose the View menu.

3. Choose Sort by.

4. From the Sort By dialog box, select to sort by Name, Type, SiZe, or Last Modification Date.

5. If you want the sort order you choose to be the default, select Set System Default.

6. Select OK to save the changes, or Cancel to abandon the changes. Press Tab until the correct button is selected, and then press Enter.

   or

   Point to the button and click the left mouse button.

To change the files that are included in the directory view

1. Open a directory (see *View a Directory*).

2. Choose the View menu.

3. Choose InClude.

4. From the Include dialog box, select Name to enter the files that you want included in the directory.

   Type *.* to include all files in the directory. Type *.TXT to include only those files in the directory that have .TXT for the extension.

5. Select the types of files to include. Choose among Directories, Programs, DocuMents, and Other Files.

6. Select Show Hidden/System Files to display files that have their Hidden or System file attributes set.

7. Select Set System Defaults to always display the directory with these options.

8. Select OK to save the changes, or Cancel to abandon the changes. Press Tab until the correct button is selected, and then press Enter.

   or

   Point to the button and click the left mouse button.

To replace each opened directory with a new directory

1. Open a directory (see *View a Directory*).

2. Choose the View menu.

3. Choose Replace on Open. If a check mark appears next to this option, directories will be replaced.

To keep directories open when opening a new directory

1. Open a directory (see *View a Directory*).

2. Choose the View menu.

3. Choose Replace on Open. When a check mark does not appear next to this option, directories will not be replaced.

Notes

When viewing files in a subdirectory, you can select how much information is viewed with each file. You can select to view only the file name. You also can select to view the file name, size, date and time of creation. Changing the directory view changes what information is displayed when you view a subdirectory. Normally, you choose to view only the file name because you can see more file names at once.

Changing View

Calendar

Purpose

Enables you to switch between viewing the calendar by day or by month.

Procedures

To view the calendar by the month

1. Choose the View menu.

2. Choose Month.

To view the calendar by the day

1. Choose the View menu.

2. Choose Day.

Notes

You may find it necessary to view an entire month at a time, but after you find the correct day, you may need to zero in on a specific day. Windows allows you to change the view of the calendar between a monthly view and a daily view.

Clipboard

Clipboard

Purpose

Stores text or graphics while they are being transferred between two applications.

Procedures

To store information in the Clipboard

1. From a Windows application, select the text or graphics to place in the Clipboard.

2. Choose the Edit menu by pressing Alt-E, or by clicking Edit with the left mouse button.

3. Choose CuT to remove the text or graphics from the application and place it in the Clipboard. Choose Copy to place a copy of the text or graphics in the Clipboard without removing the text or graphics from the application.

To open the Clipboard

1. From the Program Manager, activate the Main Program Group by opening the Window menu and choosing the number associated with Main.

2. From the Main Program Group, select Clipboard with the arrow keys and press Enter, or point to the Clipboard icon and double-click the left mouse button.

To save the Clipboard for later use

1. Start the Clipboard.

2. Choose the File menu by pressing Alt-F, or by clicking File with the left mouse button.

3. Choose Save As by pressing A, or by clicking Save As with the left mouse button.

The File Save As dialog box appears on-screen.

4. Type the new name for the file. The default extension for the file is .CLP.

5. To save the file in a different directory, choose **D**irectories by pressing **Alt-D**, then select the directory in which you want to save the file.

   If you are using a mouse, point to the correct directory and click the left mouse button.

6. Press **Tab** until the OK button is selected and press **Enter** to save the file.

   If you are using a mouse, click **OK** with the left mouse button.

   To cancel the save, press **Esc** or click **Cancel** with the left mouse button.

To open a Clipboard file

1. Start the Clipboard.

2. Choose the **F**ile menu by pressing **Alt-F**, or by clicking **File** with the left mouse button.

3. Choose **O**pen by pressing **O**, or by clicking **Open** with the left mouse button.

   The File Open dialog box appears on-screen.

4. Type the new name for the file, or choose **F**iles and select the file name of the file you want to open.

5. If you want to open a file from a different directory, choose **D**irectories by pressing **Alt-D**, then select the directory to which you want to save the file.

   If you are using a mouse, point to the directory and click the left mouse button.

6. Press **Tab** until the OK button is selected and press **Enter** to open the file.

   If you are using a mouse, click **OK** with the left mouse button.

   To cancel the file open, press **Esc** or click **Cancel** with the left mouse button.

To remove the contents of the Clipboard

1. Start the Clipboard.

2. Choose the Edit menu by pressing Alt-E, or by clicking Edit with the left mouse button.

3. Choose Delete by pressing D, or by clicking Delete with the left mouse button.

   The Clear Clipboard dialog box appears on-screen.

4. Press Enter or click OK with the left mouse button to clear the contents of the Clipboard.

   To cancel clearing, press Esc or click Cancel with the left mouse button.

To change how text is viewed in the Clipboard

1. Start the Clipboard.

2. Choose the Display menu by pressing Alt-D, or by clicking Display with the left mouse button.

3. Choose Auto by pressing A, or by clicking Auto with the left mouse button.

   The text in the Clipboard takes on the same format that it had in the originating application. You can choose one of the other options in the Display menu to vary the format of the text.

Notes

You will use Clipboard often, perhaps without realizing it. The Clipboard is used any time that you copy information between applications.

If you are using Windows in 386-Enhanced mode, you can copy information from a non-Windows application as well as Windows applications to the Clipboard. Using the Print Screen key, copy the contents of the screen to the Clipboard. You can paste the screen into the Paint accessory for printing purposes.

Clock

Accessory

Purpose

Displays the time of day.

Procedures

To start the clock using the keyboard

1. From the Program Manager, open the Accessories program group by pressing **Alt-W, 5**.

2. Press the arrow keys until Clock is selected.

3. Press **Enter** to start the clock.

To start the clock using the mouse

1. From the Program Manager, open the Accessories program group by pointing to the program group and pressing the left mouse button.

2. Double-click the **Clock** icon.

To display the clock as analog

1. Choose the **S**ettings menu.

2. Choose **A**nalog.

To display the clock as digital

1. Choose the **S**ettings menu.

2. Choose **D**igital.

Notes

An analog clock is a clock with hands. A digital clock displays digits such as 12:15. You may size the clock to be small or to take the entire screen. Even if the clock is minimized (as an icon), it displays the correct time.

Configure Serial Ports

Control Panel

Purpose

Configures any serial port so that a Windows application can communicate with a device attached to the port.

Procedure

1. From the Ports dialog box, select the correct serial port to configure using the arrow keys, or point to the serial port and click the left mouse button.

2. Press **Alt-S** or click the **Settings** button with the left mouse button.

3. From the Ports-Settings dialog box, press **Alt-B**, click the **Baud Rate** field with the left mouse button.

4. Press **Alt-down arrow**, or click the **drop-down arrow** button with the left mouse button.

5. Press the arrow keys to select the correct baud rate; then press **Alt-up arrow** to choose baud rate.

   or

   Click the correct baud rate with the left mouse button.

6. Press **Alt-D**; then press the **up-** and **down-arrow** keys to choose the correct data bits setting.

   or

   Point to one of the **Data Bits** settings and click the left mouse button.

7. Press **Alt-P**; then press the **up-** and **down-arrow** keys to choose the correct parity.

   or

   Point to one of the **Parity** settings and click the left mouse button.

8. Press **Alt-S**; then press the **up-** and **down-arrow** keys to choose **S**top Bit settings.

or

Point to one of the Stop Bits settings and click the
left mouse button.

9. Press Alt-F; then press the up- and down-arrow
   keys to choose the Flow Control settings.

   or

   Point to one of the Flow Control settings and click
   the left mouse button.

10. Press Enter or click OK with the left mouse button
    to save the changes.

    To abandon the changes, press Esc or click Cancel
    with the left mouse button.

11. From the Ports dialog box, press Enter or click OK
    with the left mouse button.

    To abandon the changes, press Esc or click Cancel
    with the left mouse button.   .

Notes

Before configuring a serial port, make sure that you
know what the settings of the serial device must be.
Consult the serial device's users manual for the proper
settings.

To configure a serial port, you first must start the
Control Panel. From the Control Panel issue the Settings
Ports command.

Copy a Disk

File Manager

Purpose

Duplicates an entire disk.

Procedure

1. Start the File Manager from the Main Program
   Group.

2. Choose the disk drivefrom which to copy by pressing **Ctrl** and the letter corresponding to the drive.

   For example, to selected drive A, press **Ctrl-A**.

   If you are using a mouse, point to the disk drive and click the left mouse button.

3. Choose the **D**isk menu.

4. Choose **C**opy Diskette.

5. From the Copy Diskette dialog box, choose Copy to continue the copy process, or Cancel to abandon the copy process. Press **Tab** to select the appropriate button, and then press **Enter**.

   or

   Point to the correct button and click the left mouse button.

6. Windows instructs you to `Please insert the source diskette into drive A`. Choose OK to continue the copy, or Cancel to abandon the copy. Press **Tab** to select the appropriate button and press **Enter**.

7. If you are prompted to change diskettes, do so and press **Enter** or click **OK** to continue the copy.

8. When the copy is complete, remove the last disk, and label the destination disk.

   You can select Cancel to abandon the copy process.

Notes

Always make backup copies of your program disks and work disks. Using File Manager's Copy Diskette function easily enables you to create disk duplicates. When duplicating a disk, you must use disks of like capacity. If the disk that you want to duplicate is a 5 1/4-inch high density disk, then the disk that you copy to must be a 5 1/4-inch high density disk.

Copy Files

File Manager

Purpose

Duplicates individual files.

Procedures

To copy file(s) from one drive to another drive using the mouse

1. Start the File Manager.

2. Place the source disk and destination disk in the correct drives.

   For example, place the source disk in drive A and the destination disk in drive B.

3. Activate the source disk clicking the **drive** icon with the left mouse button.

4. Open a window displaying the files on disk by pointing to the **drive folder** icon and double clicking the left mouse button.

   If you are going to copy the files from a subdirectory, double-click on the subdirectory with the left mouse button.

5. Click the **Directory Tree** window with the left mouse button.

6. Activate the destination drive by pointing to the correct **drive** icon and clicking the left mouse button.

7. Activate the source drive/directory window again.

8. Begin selecting the file or files to copy (see *Selecting Files*).

9. Point to the file icon of one of the selected files with the mouse, and press and hold the left mouse button.

10. Drag the Files icon to the destination drive/
directory icon. Release the mouse button after you
have the Files icon positioned over the correct
destination drive or directory icon. The Copying
dialog box appears on-screen.

You can click the Cancel button to abandon the
copy.

To copy file(s) from one drive to another drive using the keyboard

1. Start the File Manager.

2. Place the source disk and destination disk in the
correct drives. For example, place the source disk in
drive A and the destination disk in drive B.

If you are copying to or from a hard disk to a floppy
disk, place the floppy disk in the drive.

3. Activate the source disk by pressing Ctrl and the
letter associated with the drive.

For example, press Ctrl-A to activate drive A.

4. Open a window displaying the files on disk by
selecting the drive folder icon and pressing Enter.

To copy the files from a subdirectory, open the
subdirectory by pressing the up- and down-arrow
keys and pressing Enter.

5. Begin selecting the file or files you want to copy
(see *Selecting Files*).

6. Choose the File menu.

7. Choose Copy.

8. When the Copy dialog box appears, type the name
of the drive to which you want to copy.

Suppose, for example, that you are copying to a
disk in drive A. Type A:.

9. Select Copy by pressing Alt-C.

To abandon the copy process, press Tab until the
Cancel button is selected; then press Enter.

Notes

You can use the File Manager to copy files from one directory to another, from one disk to another, or between a hard disk and a floppy disk. Verify that the disk to which you want to copy has sufficient room before you start the copy procedure. If the file you are copying already exists on the disk to which you are copying, make sure that file can be overwritten. You may want to compare the file's dates and times.

Copying Program Items

Program Manager

Purpose

Duplicates a Program Item.

Procedures

To copy a program item using menus

1. Start the Program Manager.

2. Open the program group that contains the program item that you want copied. Choose the Window menu, and press the number associated with the program group.

   or

   Point to the program group and double-click the left mouse button.

3. Select the program item by pressing the **left-**, **right**, **up-**, and **down-arrow** keys.

   or

   Point to the program item and click the left mouse button.

4. Choose the File menu.

5. Choose Copy.

   The Copy Program Item dialog box appears on-screen.

6. Press Alt-T, or click the To Group field with the left mouse button.

7. Press the up- and down-arrow keys to select the correct program group, or click the drop-down list button with the mouse, and then click the correct program group with the left mouse button.

8. To complete the copy, press Enter or click OK with the left mouse button.

To copy a program item using the drag method (mouse only)

1. Start the Program Manager.

2. Open the program group that contains the program item you want to copy by double-clicking the program group with the left mouse button.

3. Point to the program item to copy, press and hold the Ctrl key and press and hold the left mouse button.

4. Drag the program item to the correct program group, then release the mouse button and the Ctrl key.

Notes

When creating new program items, you may find that the new program has similar properties to an existing program. You may copy an existing program item to another program group, then edit the copy according to the requirements of the new program. Or, you may want a program item to reside in more than one program group. In this case, you only need to copy the program item.

Create Directories

File Manager

Purpose

Enables you to create new subdirectories on your hard disk or diskette. This option is the equivalent of the DOS MD command.

To create a directory

1. Start the File Manager.

2. Select the drive you want to contain the directory by pressing **Ctrl** and the drive letter, such as **Ctrl-C** to select drive C.

   or

   Point to the drive icon with the mouse and click the left mouse button.

3. Select the directory in which you want to create a new subdirectory by pressing the **up-** and **down-arrow** keys in the Directory Tree window.

   or

   Point to the directory in the Directory Tree window and click the left mouse button. You may have to expand a directory. (See *Expanding Directory Levels*.)

4. Choose the **F**ile menu.

5. Choose Cr**E**ate Directory.

   The Create Directory dialog box appears on-screen.

   Make sure that the Create Directory box shows the correct path. Suppose, for example, that you want to create a subdirectory of C:\DATA. Make sure that C:\DATA appears in the dialog box.

6. Type the new subdirectory name, Ffor example, type **123DATA**.

7. Press **Enter** or click **OK** with the left mouse button.

   Choose the **Cancel** button to stop creating a directory.

Notes

When you create a directory, if you only type the directory name (for example NEWDIR) the directory is created as a subdirectory of the current directory. If the current directory is C:\WORD, then the new directory will be C:\WORD\NEWDIR.

If you want to create a directory in a location other than the current directory, you can choose another directory as the current directory, or you can enter the entire path for the new directory. For example, if the current directory is C:\WORD and you want NEWDIR to be a subdirectory of the C:\DATABASE directory, then type the full path **C:\DATABASE\NEWDIR**.

Date and Time Settings

Control Panel

Purpose

Sets date and time.

To change the date and time settings

1. Start the Control Panel from the Main Program Group in the Program Manager.

2. Choose Date/Time using the arrow keys and press **Enter**.

   or

   Point to the **Date/Time** icon and double-click the left mouse button.

3. Type the new month number and press **Tab**.

4. Type the day number and press **Tab**.

5. Type the new year number and press **Tab**.

6. Type the new hour number and press **Tab**.

7. Type the new minute number and press **Tab**.

8. Type the new second number and press **Tab**.

9. If the OK button is selected, press **Enter**. Otherwise, when the date and time arecorrect, click **OK** with the left mouse button.

   You can select **Cancel** to abandon the changes made to the time.

Note

You can correct the date and time settings with this option. This procedure keeps you from leaving Windows to set the date and time in DOS.

Delete a Print Job

Print Manager

Purpose

Abandons a print job being printed on the printer or in line to be printed.

Procedure

1. If the application is sending data to the Print Manager, choose the Cancel button in the printing dialog box.

2. Maximize the Print Manager by pressing **Alt-Tab** until the Print Manager is selected. Then release both keys. When you release the Alt key, the Print Manager will maximize.

   If you are using a mouse, point to the Print Manager and double-click the left mouse button.

2. Press the **up-** and **down-arrow** keys to select the print job to delete.

   or

Point to the job with the mouse, and press the left mouse button.

3. Choose the Delete button by pressing Alt-D, or by clicking Delete with the left mouse button.

Notes

As you are printing through Windows, you may notice that your print job is not printing quite right. Rather than continuing printing, or just pausing the print job, you may need to abandon the print job, deleting it from the Print Manager. Any data that has already been sent to the printer will continue.

Delete Files

File Manager

Purpose

Enables you to delete files from a disk.

Procedures

To enable or disable delete confirmation

1. From the File Manager, choose the Options menu.

2. Choose Confirmation.

   The Confirmation dialog box appears on-screen.

   Choosing Confirm on Delete toggles whether or not a dialog box appears when you delete a file or subdirectory.

3. After you make the desired settings, choose the OK button by pressing Tab and press Enter, or click OK with the left mouse button.

To delete a file or subdirectory

1. Press Ctrl and the letter of the drive that contains the file you want to delete. Suppose, for example, that you want to delete a file from drive C. Press Ctrl-C.

If you are using a mouse, point to the disk drive icon with the mouse and click the left mouse button.

2. Press the arrow keys to select the subdirectory you want to delete and press **Enter**, or point to the subdirectory and click the left mouse button.

   If the subdirectory window contains additional subdirectories that need to be opened, repeat this step.

3. Select the files to delete (see *Selecting Files*).

4. Choose the File menu by pressing **Alt-F**, or by clicking the **File** menu with the left mouse button.

5. Choose **D**elete by pressing **D**, or clicking **Delete** with the left mouse button.

   The Delete dialog box appears on-screen.

6. If the file shown in the Delete field is correct, choose Delete by pressing **Enter**, or by clicking **OK** with the left mouse button.

   To abandon delete, choose Cancel by pressing **Esc**, or by clicking **Cancel** with the left mouse button.

7. The File Manager dialog box appears so that you can verify that you really want to delete the file. Select Yes to delete the file by pressing **Y**, or by clicking **Yes** with the left mouse button.

   Select No or Cancel to abandon the operation by pressing **N** or **Esc** or by clicking either the **No** or **Cancel** buttons with the left mouse button.

Notes

When you no longer need a file or need to make room on a disk, you can delete unnecessary files. Windows enables you to select files for deletion even if their names have nothing in common.

Deleting Appointments

Calendar

Purpose

Enables you to delete appointments. You may need to
delete an appointment because it has been cancelled.
You also may decide to make deletions to make your
appointment file smaller by removing old, completed
appointments.

Procedures

To delete an appointment

1. Start the Calendar accessory.

2. Retrieve the appointment file if necessary using the
   File Open command.

3. Select the day from which you want to remove an
   appointment by pressing **Ctrl-PgUp** or **Ctrl-PgDn**,
   or click the left or right scroll bar arrows with the
   left mouse button.

4. Press the **up-** and **down-arrow** keys to select the
   appointment time to delete, or click the
   appointment time with the left mouse button.

5. Select the appointment memo by pressing **Home**,
   Ctrl-End.

   or

   Position the I-Beam at the front of the memo, press
   and hold the left mouse button, then drag the mouse
   until the memo is selected. Release the mouse
   button.

6. Delete the selected text by pressing **Backspace** or
   Del, or choose the Edit menu, then choose CuT.

To remove old appointments

1. Start the Calendar accessory.

2. Retrieve the appointment file if necessary using the
   File Open command.

3. Choose the Edit menu by pressing **Alt-E** or by
   clicking the **Edit** menu with the left mouse button.

4. Choose **R**emove by pressing **R**, or by clicking **Remove** with the left mouse button.

   The Remove dialog box appears on-screen.

5. Type a new date in the **F**rom date field, or leave the date as 1/1/80 to delete from the beginning of the file.

6. Select the **T**o date field by pressing **Alt-T**, or by clicking the **To field** with the left mouse button.

7. Type a new date in the **T**o date field.

   For example, if you want to delete from the beginning of the file to July 7, 1990, type **7/7/90** in the To field.

8. Choose OK by pressing **Enter** or clicking **OK** with the left mouse button.

   If you want to abandon this procedure, press **Esc** or click **Cancel** with the left mouse button.

Deleting Cards

Cardfile

Purpose

Enables you to delete cards that are old and no longer needed.

Procedure

1. Start the Cardfile accessory.

2. Retrieve the Card file from the disk if necessary with the **F**ile **O**pen command.

3. Use the **S**earch **G**oto command or the **S**earch **F**ind command to make the card you want deleted the current card.

4. Choose the **C**ard menu by pressing **Alt-C**, or by clicking the **Card** menu with the left mouse button.

5. Choose **D**elete by pressing **D**, or by clicking **Delete** with the left mouse button.

The Cardfile dialog box appears on-screen.

6. To confirm deletion of the card, choose OK by pressing **Enter** or by clicking **OK** with the left mouse button.

   If you want to abandon this procedure, press **Esc** or click **Cancel** with the left mouse button.

Notes

Before deleting a card from the card file, make sure that you completely review the card so that you don't delete information you may need.

You also should copy the card file to another disk for backup purposes.

Deleting Program Groups

Program Manager

Purpose

Deletes a Program Group and its associated icon from the Program Manager.

Procedure

1. Activate the Program Manager.

2. Choose the **W**indow menu by pressing **Alt-W** or by clicking the **Window** menu with the left mouse button.

3. Choose the numbered option associated with the Program Group you want to delete by pressing the option number or by pointing to the option and clicking the left mouse button.

4. Minimize the Program Group window by choosing the Program Group's control menu. Then choose MiNimize, or click the **Minimize** button with the left mouse button.

5. Choose the **F**ile menu by pressing **Alt-F** or by clicking the **File** menu with the left mouse button.

6. Choose Delete by pressing **D**, or by clicking **Delete** with the left mouse button.

   The Delete dialog box appears on-screen.

7. Confirm the deletion by choosing Yes by pressing **Y** or by clicking **Yes**.

   You can choose not to complete the deletion by pressing **N** or clicking **No**.

Note

You must use caution when deleting a Program Group. If there are any Program Items contained in the Program Group, they will be deleted as well.

Deleting Program Items

Program Manager

Purpose

Removes a Program Item from a Program Group when you no longer use an application.

Procedure

1. Activate the Program Manager.

2. Choose the **W**indow menu by pressing **Alt-W** or by clicking the **W**indow menu with the left mouse button.

3. Choose the numbered option associated with the Program Group that contains the Program Item you want to delete by pressing the option number or by pointing to the option and clicking the left mouse button.

4. Select the Program Item to delete by pressing the arrow keys or by clicking on the Program Item with the left mouse button.

5. Choose the **F**ile menu by pressing **Alt-F**, or by clicking the **F**ile menu with the left mouse button.

6. Choose Delete by pressing D, or by clicking Delete with the left mouse button.

   The Delete dialog box appears on-screen.

7. To confirm the deletion, choose Yes by pressing Y, or by clicking Yes with the left mouse button.

   You can choose not to complete the deletion with the No button. Press N or click No.

Notes

Use care when deleting a Program Item. Although you can retrieve a Program Item, you will save yourself time and frustration by making sure the correct Program Item is selected for deletion.

Desktop Customization

Control Panel

Purpose

Enables you to use several options to customize the Desktop. You can change the pattern of the Desktop, or attach a bitmapped file as "wallpaper." You also can customize the blinkrate of the cursor. Use this option to change the spacing of icons in the Program Manager. Finally, you can change the size of each window's border, and the grid for sizing windows.

Procedures

To change the Desktop pattern

1. From the Control Panel, open Desktop using Settings, Desktop, or double-click the Desktop icon with the left mouse button.

2. From the Desktop dialog box, choose Pattern Name by pressing Alt-N or by clicking the Name field with the left mouse button.

3. To view the available patterns, choose the drop-down list box by pressing Alt-down arrow, or by clicking the drop-down list box with the left mouse button.

The default patterns that you can select are as follows:

None	50% Gray
Boxes	Critters
Diamonds	Paisley
Quilt	Scottie
Spinne	Thatches
Tulip	Waffle
Weave	

4. To select the desired pattern, press the **up-** and **down-arrow** keys and then press **Alt-up-arrow**.

   or

   Click the scroll bar until the desired pattern is in view, point to the pattern and click the left mouse button.

To add a new Desktop pattern (mouse only)

1. From the Desktop dialog box, click **Edit Pattern** with the left mouse button.

2. Click the drop-down list box to select the pattern that may be similar to the pattern that you want to add, and click the pattern name.

3. Type the new pattern name.

4. Point to the pattern box and begin clicking the left mouse button to change the pattern.

5. Click the **Add** button to save the changes to the new pattern name.

6. Click **OK** to save the new pattern. Click **Cancel** to abandon the new pattern.

To edit the Desktop pattern (mouse only)

1. From the Desktop dialog box, click **Edit Pattern** with the left mouse button.

2. Click the drop-down list box to select the pattern to edit, and click the pattern name.

3. Point to the pattern box and begin clicking the left mouse button to change the pattern.

4. Click the Change button to save the changes to the assigned name.

5. Click OK to save the changes to the pattern. Click Cancel to abandon the pattern changes.

To remove a Desktop pattern

1. From the Desktop dialog box, choose Edit Pattern by pressing Alt-P, or by clicking the Edit Pattern with the left mouse button.

2. Choose the drop-down list box by pressing Alt-down arrow, or by clicking the drop-down list box. Select the pattern you want to remove by using the arrow keys or by clicking the pattern name.

5. Choose the Remove button by pressing Alt-R, or by clicking Remove with the left mouse button.

6. Choose OK by pressing Enter or by clicking OK with the left mouse button.

Choose Cancel by pressing Esc, or clicking Cancel with the left mouse button to abandon removing the pattern.

To change the Desktop wallpaper

1. From the Desktop dialog box, select Wallpaper File by pressing Alt-F, or by clicking the File field with the left mouse button.

2. Choose the File drop-down list box by pressing Alt-down arrow, or by clicking the drop-down list box with the left mouse button.

3. To choose the wallpaper file, press the arrow keys and then press Alt-up arrow.

or

Point to the wallpaper file and click the left mouse button.

4. To place the wallpaper in the center of the screen, select Center by pressing Alt-C, or by clicking Center with the left mouse button.

5. To place the wallpaper side-by-side on the screen, select Tile by pressing Alt-T, or by clicking Tile with the left mouse button.

To change the cursor blink rate

1. From the Desktop dialog box, select Cursor Blink
   Rate by pressing Alt-R, or by clicking the Cursor
   Blink Rate scroll bar with the left mouse button.

2. Change the blink rate in one of these ways:

   • Press the right and left arrow keys.
   • Point to the scroll box with the mouse, press and
     hold the left mouse button, drag the scroll box to
     the desired position, and release the left mouse
     button.
   • Point to the scroll arrows with the mouse and
     click the left mouse button until the scroll box is
     in the desired position.
   As you adjust the position of the scroll box, the
   gray shadow blinks at the rate that the cursor will
   blink.

To change the icon spacing

1. From the Desktop dialog box, select Icon Spacing
   by pressing Alt-I, or by clicking the Icon Spacing
   field with the left mouse button.

2. Change the Icon Spacing to a pixel value between
   32 and 512 by typing the new number, or by
   pointing to the scroll arrows with the mouse and
   clicking the left mouse button until the desired
   number appears in the field.

To change the grid on which a window is sized

1. From the Desktop dialog box, select Granularity by
   pressing Alt-G, or by clicking the Granularity
   field with the left mouse button.

2. Change the Granularity to a value between 0 and 49
   by typing the new number, or by pointing to the
   scroll arrows with the mouse and clicking the left
   mouse button until the desired number appears in
   the field.

To change the border width

1. From the Desktop dialog box, select Border Width
   by pressing Alt-B, or by clicking the Border
   Width field with the left mouse button.

2. Change the Granularity to a value between 1 and 49
   by typing the new number, or by pointing to the

scroll arrows with the mouse and clicking the left
mouse button until the desired number appears in
the field.

Notes

You can experiment with the options that may be
customized on the Desktop. Although these options
change many features of Windows' Desktop, nothing
that you change causes adverse consequences. Each
option, when modified, may be returned to its original
setting.

Before you change any of the Desktop options, you first
must start the Control Panel, choose the Settings menu,
and then choose the Desktop option.

Directory Tree Usage

File Manager

Purpose

Lists all the subdirectories on the current disk drive.
From the Directory Tree window, you can expand and
collapse each subdirectory branch. In addition, you can
open a subdirectory window (folder) so that you see all
the subdirectories and files that the subdirectory
contains.

Procedures

To select a disk drive

To select a different disk drive, press **Ctrl** and the letter
that corresponds to the disk drive. Suppose, for example,
that you want to select disk drive A. Press **Ctrl-A**.

If you are using a mouse, point to the disk drive icon and
click the left mouse button.

To select a subdirectory using the keyboard

With the Directory Tree window active, press the **up-**
and **down-arrow** keys to move the highlight to the
correct subdirectory. The window will scroll as
necessary.

To select a subdirectory using the mouse

1. Activate the Directory Tree window. Press and hold the left mouse button and drag the scroll box until the desired subdirectory is in view. Release the mouse button.

2. Point to the desired subdirectory with the mouse and click the left mouse button.

To expand one level of a subdirectory branch using the keyboard

1. With the Directory Tree window active, select the subdirectory whose branch needs to be expanded one level.

2. Choose the Tree menu by pressing Alt-T.

3. Choose Expand One Level by pressing E.

To expand one level of a subdirectory branch using the mouse

1. With the Directory Tree window active, point to the scroll box with the mouse, press and hold the left mouse button and drag the scroll box until the desired subdirectory is in view. Release the mouse button.

2. Point to the desired subdirectory whose icon contains a plus and click the left mouse button.

To expand an entire subdirectory branch

1. With the Directory Tree window active, select the subdirectory whose branch needs to be expanded.

2. Choose the Tree menu by pressing Alt-T, or by clicking the Tree menu with the left mouse button.

3. Choose Expand Branch by pressing B, or by clicking Expand Branch with the left mouse button.

To expand all subdirectory branches

1. With the Directory Tree window active, select the subdirectory whose branch needs to be expanded.

2. Choose the Tree menu by pressing Alt-T, or by clicking the Tree menu with the left mouse button.

3. Choose Expand All by pressing **A**, or by clicking **Expand All** with the left mouse button.

To collapse an entire subdirectory branch

1. With the Directory Tree window active, select the subdirectory whose branch needs to be Collapsed.

2. Choose the Tree menu by pressing **Alt-T**, or by clicking the **Tree** menu with the left mouse button.

3. Choose Collapse Branch by pressing **C**, or by clicking **Collapse Branch** with the left mouse button.

Notes

The Directory Tree window is the main window that you use, and the first window that you see when you start the File Manager.

Subdirectories are among the hardest concepts for most new users to grasp. However, using the Directory Tree window, you can see what a subdirectory does, and where each subdirectory actually resides in relation to other subdirectories.

If you do not see a subdirectory that you think should be displayed in the Directory Tree window, a subdirectory branch may be collapsed, displaying only the upper-level subdirectory. You may have to use the scroll bars to view additional subdirectories and subdirectory branches.

Drive Selection

File Manager

Purpose

Selects a disk drive so that you can examine a Directory Tree of a disk drive other than the current disk drive.

Procedure

To select a different disk drive, press the **Ctrl** key and the letter that corresponds to the disk drive. For example, to select disk drive A, press **Ctrl-A**. If you are using the mouse, point to the disk drive icon and click the left mouse button.

Editing Cards

Cardfile

Purpose

Enables you to change information on a Cardfile when you work with any database.

Procedures

To change current information on a card

1. Start the Cardfile accessory.

2. Retrieve the Cardfile from the disk with the File Open command.

3. Make the card you want to edit the current card by using the Search Goto command or the Search Find command.

4. Use the arrow keys to position the cursor on the card on which you want to add or change information.

   or

   Point to the location on the card and click the left mouse button.

5. Select any information you want replaced and type the new information.

6. Be sure that you save the Cardfile with the File Save command.

To add new information to a card

1. Start the Cardfile accessory.

2. If necessary, retrieve the Cardfile from the disk with the File Open command.

3. Make the card you want to edit the current card. by using the Search Goto command or the Search Find command.

4. Use the arrow keys to position the cursor on the card on which you want to change or add information.

   or

   Point to the location on the card and click the left mouse button.

5. Begin typing the new information.

6. Be sure that you save the Cardfile using the File Save command.

Note

Anytime you change information on a card, and save the information, the previous information is lost. If you feel that you may need this information, add the new information to the card, or copy the Cardfile before you make any changes.

Editing Notes

Notepad

Purpose

Enables you to make changes to existing text in a notepad file.

Procedure

1. Start the Notepad accessory.

2. Retrieve the file you want to edit from disk using the File Open command.

3. Place the cursor in the desired location by pressing the arrow keys.

   or

   Move the mouse until the I-beam bar is at the desired location, then click the left mouse button.

   If you are replacing text, select the text to replace.

4. Begin typing the text. Be sure to save the document after you make changes using File Save or File Save As.

Note

Editing is a large part of any text editing program. Be careful when you make changes to a document. Saving the changes erases the original text. Before making changes to a document, you may want to make a copy of the original document.

Expanding Directory Levels

File Manager

Purpose

Modifies the Directory Tree window so that you can see all subdirectories, or only levels of subdirectories. Expand directory levels to view more than just first level directories.

Procedures

To expand one level of a subdirectory branch using the keyboard

1. With the Directory Tree window active, select the subdirectory whose branch needs to be expanded one level.

2. Choose the Tree menu by pressing Alt-T.

3. Choose Expand One Level by pressing E.

To expand one level of a subdirectory branch using the mouse

1. With the Directory Tree window active, point to the scroll box with the mouse, press and hold the left mouse button and drag the scroll box until the desired subdirectory is in view. Release the mouse button.

2. Point to the desired subdirectory whose icon contains a plus and click the left mouse button.

To expand an entire subdirectory branch

1. With the Directory Tree window active, select the subdirectory whose branch needs to be expanded.

2. Choose the Tree menu by pressing **Alt-T**, or by clicking **Tree** menu with the left mouse button.

3. Choose Expand **B**ranch by pressing **B**.

To expand all subdirectory branches

1. With the Directory Tree window active, select the subdirectory whose branch needs to be expanded.

2. Choose the Tree menu by pressing **Alt-T**, or by clicking the **Tree** menu with the left mouse button.

3. Choose Expand **A**ll by pressing **A**.

Font Selection

Control Panel

Purpose

Enables you to add and remove fonts from the operating environment. Windows is a *what you see is what you get* environment. That is, what you see on-screen basically is what you will see on the printed page. Programs written to take advantage of the Windows environment can access these fonts, whereas non-Windows programs are not designed to. You must be able to see different fonts on screen, however. A font is a combination typeface and typesize of the characters that you use in a document.

Procedures

To add fonts to Windows

1. From the Fonts dialog box, choose **A**dd by pressing **Alt-A**, or by clicking **Add** with the left mouse button.

2. When the Add Font Files dialog box appears, press **Alt-D** to choose directories, press the arrow keys to select the correct drive and directory, and press **Enter**.

or

Point to the correct drive or directory and click the left mouse button.

3. Select Font Files by pressing **Alt-F**, press the arrow keys to select the font files (pressing the space bar if the select bar is an outline rather than a highlight), and press **Enter**.

   If you are using a mouse, point to the correct font file and double-click the left mouse button. If the font is already installed, then a message dialog box appears and you see `Font already installed`.

   Press **Enter** or click **OK** to continue.

4. Choose OK by pressing **Enter** or clicking **OK** with the left mouse button.

To remove fonts from Windows

1. From the Fonts dialog box, press **Alt-F**, using the arrow keys to select the font to remove.

   If you are using a mouse, point to the font you want to remove and click the left mouse button.

2. Choose **R**emove by pressing **Alt-R**, or by clicking **Remove** with the left mouse button.

   The Control Panel dialog box appears on-screen.

3. Choose **Y**es to remove the font by pressing **Y**, or click the **Yes** button with the left mouse button.

   To abandon this procedure, choose **N**o by pressing **N**, or by clicking the **N**o button with the left mouse button.

4. Choose OK by pressing **Enter** or clicking the **OK** button with the left mouse button.

Notes

Windows can support different fonts, and you may find that you want to add fonts to the operating environment. Note that when you add a font to Windows, you use disk space. If you are running short on disk space, you can temporarily remove fonts that you use on a non-continuous basis. Before you change any of the font

options, you first must start the Control Panel, then
choose the Settings menu, and choose the Fonts option.

Format a Disk

File Manager

Purpose

Prepares a new disk for use with the computer.

Procedure

1. Start the File Manager application.

2. Choose the Disk menu by pressing **Alt-D**, or by
   clicking the **Disk** menu with the left mouse button.

3. Choose Format Diskette by pressing **F**, or by
   clicking **Format Diskette** with the left mouse
   button.

   The Format Diskette dialog box appears on-screen.

4. Choose the Disk drop-down list box by pressing
   Alt-down arrow, or by clicking the **Disk** drop-
   down list box with the left mouse button.

   The list of diskette drives appears.

5. To choose the drive you want to format press the
   arrow keys and press **Enter**.

   or

   Click the drive to format with the left mouse button.

6. After you select the drive, press **Enter** or click **OK**
   with the left mouse button.

   To abandon the diskette format, press **Esc** or click
   Cancel with the left mouse button.

7. The message `Formatting will erase ALL`
   `data from your diskette. Are you`
   `sure you want to format the`
   `diskette in Drive A:?` appears in the
   Format Diskette dialog box if you chose to format a
   disk in drive A. To continue, press **Enter** or **F** to

choose Format, or click **Format** with the left mouse button.

To cancel the diskette format, press **Esc** or click **Cancel** with the left mouse button.

8. The message `Please insert the diskette to format into Drive A:` appears. If you selected drive B, then the message indicates so. Place the disk to format in the correct drive, and close the drive door if there is one to close.

   The Format Diskette dialog box contains two options. These two options toggle whether the diskette you are formatting is a High Capacity diskette (also called high density), and whether you want to Make System Disk so that you can start the computer using the diskette. If the High Capacity box is marked, then you are formatting a high capacity diskette. If the Make System Disk box is marked, then the DOS files will be transferred to the diskette after it is formatted.

9. Select High Capacity by pressing **H** or by clicking the **High Capacity** box with the left mouse button. This is a toggle.

10. Select **M**ake System Disk by pressing **M** or by clicking the **Make System Disk** box with the left mouse button. This is a toggle.

11. Select OK by pressing **Enter** or by clicking **OK** with the left mouse button.

    To cancel formatting, press **Esc** or click **Cancel** with the left mouse button. The Format Diskette dialog box displays the percentage of the disk that has been formatted.

    You can press **Esc** to abort the format, or click **Cancel** with the left mouse button.

12. The Format Complete dialog box appears with the message, `Do you want to format another diskette?` Choose **Y**es by pressing **Y**, and choose No by pressing **N** or **Esc**. If you choose Yes, you return to Step 7.

Note

If your computer has more than one disk drive, be sure
that you choose the correct drive to format. If your
computer has a high-density drive, verify whether you
are formatting a double-density or high-density drive.

Hardware Settings

Setup

Purpose

Changes Windows so that it adapts to new hardware.
When you add new hardware, Windows needs
adjustment for the display, keyboard, mouse, and
network.

Procedures

To change the type of display

1. From the Windows Setup dialog box, choose the
   Options menu by pressing Alt-O, or by clicking
   Options with the left mouse button.

2. Choose Change System Settings by pressing C, or
   clicking Change System Settings with the left
   mouse button.

3. From the Change System Settings dialog box,
   choose Display by pressing Alt-D, or by clicking
   the Display field with the left mouse button.

4. Choose the drop-down list box by pressing Alt-
   down arrow, or by clicking the drop-down list box
   with the left mouse button.

5. Use the arrow keys to select the correct type and
   press Enter.

   If you are using a mouse, use the scroll bar to find
   the correct display, and choose the correct display
   type by pointing to the display type and clicking the
   left mouse button.

6. Choose OK by pressing Enter or by clicking OK with the left mouse button.

To change the type of keyboard

1. From the Windows Setup dialog box, choose the Options menu by pressing Alt-O, or by clicking Options with the left mouse button.

2. Choose Change System Settings by pressing C, or clicking Change System Settings with the left mouse button.

3. From the Change System Settings dialog box, choose Keyboard by pressing Alt-K, or by clicking the Keyboard field with the left mouse button.

4. Choose the drop-down list box by pressing Alt-down arrow or by clicking the drop-down list box with the left mouse button.

5. Press the arrow keys to choose the correct keyboard type and press Enter.

   If you are using a mouse, use the scroll bar to find the correct keyboard, and click the keyboard type with the left mouse button.

6. Choose OK by pressing Enter or by clicking OK with the left mouse button.

To change the type of mouse

1. From the Windows Setup dialog box, choose the Options menu by pressing Alt-O, or by clicking Options with the left mouse button.

2. Choose Change System Settings by pressing C, or clicking Change System Settings with the left mouse button.

3. From the Change System Settings dialog box, choose Mouse by pressing Alt-M, or by clicking the Mouse field with the left mouse button.

4. Choose the drop-down list box by pressing Alt-down arrow, or by clicking the drop-down list box with the left mouse button.

5. Press the arrow keys to select the correct mouse
   type and press Enter.

   or

   Use the scroll bar to find the correct mouse, and
   click the mouse type with the left mouse button.

6. Choose OK by pressing Enter or by clicking OK
   with the left mouse button.

To change the type of network

1. From the Windows Setup dialog box, choose the
   Options menu by pressing Alt-O, or by clicking
   Options with the left mouse button.

2. Choose Change System Settings by pressing C, or
   clicking Change System Settings with the left
   mouse button.

3. From the Change System Settings dialog box,
   choose Network by pressing Alt-N, or by clicking
   the Network field with the left mouse button.

4. Choose the drop-down list box by pressing Alt-
   down arrow, or by clicking the drop-down list box
   with the left mouse button.

5. Use the arrow keys to select the correct network
   type and press Enter.

   If you are using a mouse, use the scroll bar to find
   the correct network, and then click the left mouse
   button.

6. Choose OK by pressing Enter or by clicking OK
   with the left mouse button.

Notes

When you make changes to the Windows setup, make
sure that you select the correct devices. Selecting an
incorrect device may cause Windows to function
improperly or not function at all.

To change any hardware settings, you must start
Windows Setup from the Main program group in the
Program Manager.

Help

General

Purpose

Displays context-sensitive help.

Procedures

To get the help index

1. Choose the Help menu.

2. Choose Index. The Help window appears on-screen.

To get help on the keyboard

1. Choose the Help menu.

2. Choose Keyboard. The Help window appears on-screen.

To get help on commands

1. Choose the Help menu.

2. Choose Commands. The Help window appears on-screen.

To get help on procedures

1. Choose the Help menu.

2. Choose Procedures. The Help window appears on-screen.

To get help on help

1. Choose the Help menu.

2. Choose Help. The Help window appears on-screen.

To open a new help file

1. Choose the File menu.

2. Choose Open. The File Open dialog box appears on the screen.

3. Choose Directories by pressing Alt-D, then change to the Windows subdirectory. If you are using a mouse, point to the correct directory and double-click the left mouse button to change directories.

4. Choose Files.

5. Select the correct help file using the **up-** and **down-arrow** keys, or by pointing to the help file with the mouse and clicking the left mouse button.

6. Choose the Open button by pressing Enter, or by clicking the **Open** button with the left mouse button. To abandon opening a file, press Esc or click Cancel with the left mouse button.

To print a help topic

1. Select the appropriate help topic.

2. Choose the File menu.

3. Choose Print Topic.

4. When the Print dialog box appears on-screen, you may press Esc or click Cancel button with left mouse button to abandon the printing.

To add notes to a help topic

1. Select the appropriate help topic.

2. Choose the Edit menu.

3. Choose Annotate.

4. When the Help Annotate dialog box appears, choose Annotation by pressing Alt-A, or by clicking the Annotation field with the left mouse button.

5. Begin typing the notes to remember.

6. Press Enter or click OK with the left mouse button to save the Annotation. To abandon the annotation, press Esc or click Cancel with the left mouse button. A paper clip icon will appear in the help window.

To view an annotation using the keyboard

1. Select the help topic containing the annotation (a paper clip will appear in the help window).

2. Choose the Edit menu.

3. Choose Annotate. The note that you previously typed will appear in the Help Annotation dialog box.

To view an annotation using the mouse

1. Select the help topic containing the annotation (a paper clip will appear in the help window).

2. Point to the paper clip icon and click the left mouse button.

To delete an annotation

1. Select the help topic containing the annotation (a paper clip will appear in the help window).

2. Choose the Edit menu.

3. Choose Annotate. The Help Annotation dialog box appears on-screen.

4. Choose Delete by pressing Alt-D, or by clicking the Delete button with the left mouse button.

To insert a bookmark in a help topic

1. Select the help topic.

2. Choose the BookMark menu.

3. Choose Define. The Bookmark Define dialog box appears on-screen.

4. Choose Bookmark Name by pressing Alt-B, or by clicking the Bookmark Name field with the left mouse button.

5. Leave the default bookmark name as is or type a new bookmark name.

6. Press Enter or click OK with the left mouse button to accept the bookmark. Press Esc or click Cancel button with the left mouse button to abandon the bookmark.

To choose a bookmark in a help topic

1. Select Help.

2. Choose the BookMark menu.

3. Choose the bookmark name from the menu by pressing the number associated to the bookmark name, or by pointing to the bookmark name and clicking the left mouse button.

To delete a bookmark in a help topic

1. Select the help topic.

2. Choose the BookMark menu.

3. Choose Define. The Bookmark Define dialog box appears on-screen.

4. Select the bookmark to delete by pressing Tab, and using the arrow keys highlight the bookmark to delete. If you are using a mouse, point to the bookmark and click the left mouse button.

5. Choose Delete by pressing Alt-D, or by clicking the Delete button and clicking the left mouse button.

To get the help index for the topic

From the help window, choose Index by pressing Alt-I, or by clicking Index with the left mouse button.

To back up to the last help text

From the help window, choose Back by pressing Alt-B, or by clicking the Back button with the left mouse button.

To browse through the help topics

From the help window, choose BRowse or BrOwse by pressing Alt-R or Alt-O by clicking on the Browse buttons with the left mouse button.

To search for a help topic

1. From the help window, choose Search by pressing Alt-S, or by clicking the Search button with the left mouse button. The Search dialog box appears on the screen.

2. Choose Search For by pressing Alt-S, or by clicking the Search For field with the left mouse button.

3. Begin typing the topic to search for. As you begin typing text, topics in the next window will become selected.

4. When the correct topic is selected, choose Search by pressing **Enter**, or by clicking the **Search** with the left mouse button.

5. Choose Topics Found.

6. Select the correct topic using the **up-** and **down-arrow** keys, or by pointing to the topic and clicking the left mouse button.

7. Choose the **Go** To button by pressing **Alt-G**, or by pointing to the button and clicking the left mouse button.

Icon Selection

General

Purpose

Enables you to select icons so that you can open, delete, copy, or manipulate a file or application.

Procedures

To select a Program Group icon with the keyboard

1. Activate the Program Manager.

2. Choose the **W**indow menu by pressing **Alt-W**.

3. Choose the number associated with the Program Group icon. For example, if the Accessories Program Group icon is number 5, and you want to select the Accessories icon, you press **5**.

To select a Program Group icon with the mouse

1. Activate the Program Manager.

2. Point to the correct Program Group icon and click the left mouse button.

To select a Program Item icon with the keyboard

1. Activate the Program Manager.

2. Open the correct Program Group icon.

3. Using the arrow keys, highlight the correct Program Group icon.

To select a Program Item icon with the mouse

1. Activate the Program Manager.

2. Open the correct Program Group icon.

3. Point to the correct Program Group icon and click the left mouse button.

Note

Make sure that you select the correct icon. You normally select an icon when you want to copy it, move it, change its properties, or affect it in some other way. Selecting the wrong icon may cause you to effect the wrong icon.

International Options

Control Panel

Purpose

Enables you to operate Windows with the rules for a different country. The following countries are available: Australia, Austria, Belgium (Dutch), Belgium (French), Brazil, Canada (English), Canada (French), Norway, Portugal, South Korea, Spain, Sweden, Switzerland (French), Switzerland (German), Switzerland (Italian), Taiwan, United Kingdom, and the United States. The default country is the United States.

Procedures

To change the country

1. Choose Country by pressing Alt-C, or by clicking the Country field with the left mouse button.

2. Choose the drop-down list box by pressing **Alt-down arrow,** or by clicking the drop-down list box with the left mouse button.

3. From the list of countries, choose the correct country by using the arrow keys and then press **Enter**.

   If you are using a mouse, use the scroll bars until the correct country is in view, then point to the country and click the left mouse button.

   When you select the country, all items in the International dialog box change with the exception of Language and Keyboard Layout.

To change the language

1. Choose Language by pressing **Alt-L**, or by clicking the **Language** field with the left mouse button.

2. Choose the drop-down list box by pressing **Alt-down arrow**, or by clicking the drop-down list box with the left mouse button.

3. From the list of languages, choose the correct language by using the arrow keys and then press **Enter**.

   If you are using a mouse, use the scroll bars until the correct language is in view, then point to the language and click the left mouse button. Make sure the language matches all the other country settings.

   For example, if you chose the country Sweden, then you should choose the Swedish language.

To change the keyboard layout

1. Choose Keyboard Layout by pressing **Alt-K**, or by clicking the **Keyboard Layout** field with the left mouse button.

2. Choose the drop-down list box by pressing **Alt-down arrow**, or by clicking the drop-down list box with the left mouse button.

3. From the list of keyboard layouts, choose the correct layout by using the arrow keys and then press **Enter**.

If you are using a mouse, use the scroll bars until
the correct layout is in view, then point to the
keyboard layout and click the left mouse button.
Make sure that the keyboard layout matches all the
other country settings.

For example, if you chose the country Sweden and
the language as Swedish, then choose the Swedish
keyboard layout.

To change the measurement

1. Choose Measurement by pressing **Alt-M**, or by
   clicking the **Measurement** field with the left mouse
   button.

2. Choose the drop-down list box by pressing **Alt-
   down arrow**, or by clicking the drop-down list box
   with the left mouse button.

3. From the list of measurements, choose the correct
   measurement by using the arrow keys then press
   Enter. You have the choice of choosing Metric or
   English.

   If you are using a mouse, use the scroll bars until
   the correct measurement is in view, then point to
   the measurement and click the left mouse button.

   Make sure that the measurement matches all the
   other country settings.

To change the list separator

1. Choose List Separator by pressing **Alt-P**, or by
   clicking the **List Separator** field with the left
   mouse button.

2. Type the correct list separator. Make sure that the
   measurement matches all the other country settings.

To change the date format

1. Choose Date Format by pressing **Alt-D**, or by
   clicking the **Change** button in the **D**ate Format area
   with the left mouse button.

2. Choose the Short Date Format Order by pressing
   Alt-O, and then press the **left-** and **right-arrow**
   keys to select MDY, DMY, or YMD.

If you are using a mouse, point to either MDY, DMY, or YMD with the mouse button and click the left mouse button.

3. Choose the Short Date Format Separator by pressing **Alt-S**, or by clicking the **Short Date Format Separator** field with the left mouse button.

4. Type the correct Separator character.

   Americans use the comma and Europeans use a period as a separator character.

5. Choose Short Date Format **D**ay Leading Zero to begin the day number with a zero. Press **Alt-D**, or click the **Day Leading Zero** box with the left mouse button.

6. Choose Short Date Format **M**onth Leading Zero to begin the month number with a zero. Press **Alt-M** or click the **Month Leading Zero** box with the left mouse button.

7. Choose Short Date Format **C**entury to specify whether the century begins with two digits or four. Press **Alt-C**, or click the **Century** box with the left mouse button.

8. Choose the Long Date Format O**R**der by pressing **Alt-R**, and then press the **left-** and **right-arrow** keys to select MDY, DMY, YMD formats.

   If you are using a mouse, point to either MDY, DMY, or YMD and click the left mouse button.

9. Press **Tab** to choose whether to display the day name. Press **Alt-down arrow**, and choose from no day name, a three-letter day name, or full day name. After you make your selection, press **Alt-up arrow**.

   If you are using a mouse, click the drop-down list box, and click the day name type you want.

10. Press **Tab** to choose whether to display the day number's leading zero. Press **Alt-down arrow**. Select from no leading zero or a leading zero, and then press **Alt-up arrow**.

    If you are using a mouse, click the drop-down list box, and click the day number you want.

12. Press **Tab** to choose whether to display the month as a number with or without a leading zero, as a name with only three letters, or as the full month name. Press **Alt-down arrow**, select the correct month option, and press **Alt-up arrow**.

If you are using a mouse, click the drop-down list box, and click the month option you want.

13. Press **Tab** to choose whether to display the year with two numbers or with all four numbers. Press **Alt-down arrow**, select the correct option, and press **Alt-up arrow**.

If you are using a mouse, click the drop-down list box, and click the option you want.

14. Choose OK to accept changes to the International-Date Format by pressing **Enter** or by clicking **OK** with the left mouse button.

You can abandon the changes made to the International-Date Format by pressing **Esc** or by clicking **Cancel** with the left mouse button.

To change the time format

1. Choose Time Format by pressing **Alt-T**, or by clicking the **Change** button in the **T**ime Format area with the left mouse button.

2. Choose a 12-hour clock by pressing **Alt-2** or a 24-hour clock by pressing **Alt-4**.

If you are using a mouse, click either 12 hour or 24 hour with the left mouse button.

3. Choose Separator by pressing **Alt-S**, or by clicking the Separator field with the left mouse button. Type the separator character you want to use.

4. Choose Leading Zero by pressing **Alt-L**, and press the **right-** and **left-arrow** keys to select whether you want a leading zero used.

If you are using a mouse, point to 9:15 and click the left mouse button if you prefer not to use a leading zero. Point to 09:15 to use a leading zero, and click the left mouse button.

5. Choose OK to accept changes to the International-Time Format by pressing **Enter** or by clicking **OK** with the left mouse button.

   To abandon the changes made to the International-Time Format, press **Esc** or click **Cancel** with the left mouse button.

To change the currency format

1. Choose CUrrency Format by pressing **Alt-U**, or by clicking the **Change** button in the CUrrency Format area with the left mouse button.

2. Choose Symbol Placement by pressing **Alt-P**, or by clicking the **Symbol Placement** field with the left mouse button.

3. Choose one of the four symbol placements by pressing **Alt-down arrow**, or by clicking the **Symbol Placement** drop-down list.

   Use the arrow keys to select the correct symbol placement and press **Enter**, or click the correct symbol placement with the left mouse button.

4. Choose Negative by pressing **Alt-N**, or by clicking the **Negative** field with the left mouse button.

5. Press **Alt-down arrow**, or click the **Negative** drop-down list box with the left mouse button. Use the arrow keys to select the correct negative and press **Enter**, or point to the correct negative and click the left mouse button.

   If you are using a mouse, you may need to use the scroll bars to reveal other negative options.

6. Choose Symbol by pressing **Alt-S**, or by clicking the **Symbol** field with the left mouse button.

7. Type the correct currency symbol.

8. Choose Decimal Digits by pressing **Alt-D**, or by clicking the **Decimal Digits** field with the left mouse button.

9. Type the number of decimals that should be displayed.

10. Choose OK to accept changes to the International-Currency Format by pressing **Enter**, or by clicking **OK** with the left mouse button.

To abandon the changes made to the International-Currency Format, press **Esc** or click **Cancel** with the left mouse button.

To change the number format

1. Choose Number Format by pressing **Alt-N**, or by clicking the **Change** button in the Number Format area with the left mouse button.

2. Choose 1000 Separator by pressing **Alt-S**, or by clicking the **1000 Separator** field with the left mouse button.

3. Type the character you want to use for the 1000 separator.

4. Choose Decimal Separator by pressing **Alt-D**, or by clicking the **Decimal Separator** field with the left mouse button.

5. Type the character you want to use for the decimal separator.

6. Choose DEcimal Digits by pressing **Alt-E**, or by clicking the **Decimal Digits** field with the left mouse button.

7. Type the number of decimals that should be displayed.

8. Choose Leading Zero by pressing **Alt-L**, and press **right arrow** to use a leading zero and **left arrow** to choose not to use a leading zero.

If you are using a mouse, click .7 with the left mouse button to not use a leading zero, or click **0.7** to use a leading zero.

9. Choose OK to accept changes to the International-Number Format by pressing **Enter** or by clicking **OK** with the left mouse button.

To abandon the changes made to the International-Number Format, press **Esc** or click **Cancel** with the left mouse button.

To save all the International options

Choose OK to accept changes to the International-Number Format by pressing **Enter** or by clicking **OK** with the left mouse button.

To abandon the changes made to the International-Number Format, press **Esc** or click **Cancel** with the left mouse button.

Notes

Use the International Options to customize Windows for foreign language. Note that when you choose a country that you normally do not work with, the keyboard may be different, causing you to type incorrect information.

If you choose a foreign country, make sure that all international settings agree for that country. To change any International settings, you first must start International from the Control Panel. Start the Control Panel, and choose the Settings International command.

Keyboard Modification

Control Panel

Purpose

Enables you to change the key-repeat rate of your keyboard. You can, for example, increase or decrease the speed that your cursor moves on-screen.

Procedure

1. Choose Keyboard from the Control panel using the Settings Keyboard command, or point to the Keyboard icon and click the left mouse button.

2. Change the Key Repeat rate in one of the following ways:

   • Press the **right-** and **left-arrow** keys to move the scroll box to the desired location.

- Click the scroll arrows with the left mouse button.

- Point to the scroll box with the mouse, press and hold the left mouse button, drag the scroll box, and release the mouse button.

3. Test the repeat rate by choosing Test Typeamatic and hold a key on the keyboard.

4. Repeat Steps 2 and 3 until the desired repeat rate is attained.

Notes

When you change the rate of the keyboard, make sure that the rate is not so fast that you cannot keep up with the cursor.

The keyboard stores characters you type in a buffer so that although the computer is not yet accepting the characters, you can type ahead. If the computer begins beeping as you type, you may need to slow down the key-repeat rate. The beeping means that the buffer is full, and the keyboard is not accepting characters.

Menu Selection

General

Purpose

Enables you to use applications and perform most of the Windows operations. Because all Windows' menus operate in the same manner, menus can be classified in the same section.

Purpose

To choose a menu with the keyboard

1. Press Alt in conjunction with the underlined menu character. You can press Alt and then press the underlined menu character, or press and hold Alt, press the underlined menu character, and then

release both keys. For example, to select the File menu, you can press **Alt** and then press **F**, or press **Alt-F**.

2. Choose the menu option on the menu in one of two ways. Use the **up-** and **down-arrow** keys to select the menu option and press **Enter**, or press the underlined menu option character. For example, to select the Open menu option, press **O**.

To choose a menu with the mouse

1. Point to the menu with the mouse and press the left mouse button.

2. To choose an item on the menu, point to the menu item and click the left mouse button. Make sure that the point of the arrow is directly over the menu item.

Notes

Although Windows menus are easy to use, make sure that you completely point to the menu option you want to select before pressing the mouse button. You can corrupt or lose data if you accidentally point above or below the option that you actually want.

Each menu has a name, with one of the characters underlined. The underlined character is the character that calls the menu.

Merge Macros

Recorder

Purpose

Enables you to add macros from one or more macro files to make a single macro file.

Procedure

1. Start the Recorder accessory.

2. Open the file to which you want to merge with the File Open command.

3. Choose the File menu by pressing Alt-F, or by clicking the File menu with the left mouse button.

4. Choose Merge by pressing M, or clicking Merge options with the left mouse button.

5. Choose the correct directory from the Directories list by pressing Alt-D. Press the up- and down-arrow keys to select the correct drive and directory and press Enter.

   If you are using a mouse, point to the correct drive or directory and click the left mouse button.

6. Choose the macro file from the Files list by pressing Alt-F. Press the up- and down-arrow keys to select the correct macro file and press Enter.

   If you are using a mouse, point to the correct macro file with the mouse and click the left mouse button.

7. Choose OK to accept the merge by pressing Enter or by clicking OK with the left mouse button.

   To abandon the merge, press Esc or click Cancel with the left mouse button.

8. Be sure to save the changes. Choose the File Save As command, type a new macro file name, and choose OK to create the new macro file.

Notes

You will often keep macro files that contain macros for different operations. For example, you may create a set of macros for saving and printing. You also may have a set of macros for formatting a document in a wordprocessor, and one macro file that contains all macros to format a document in your word processor and save and print.

Minimize Windows

General

Purpose

Enables you to choose how an application appears. An application can exist in a window that takes up the entire screen or just a portion of the screen, or as an icon.

Procedures

To minimize a window using the keyboard

1. Choose the control menu by pressing **Alt-space bar**.

2. Choose MiNimize by pressing **Alt-N**. If the window occupied the entire screen, the window is reduced to occupy only a portion of the screen. If the window occupied only a portion of the screen, it is reduced to an icon.

To minimize a window using the mouse

1. Choose the control menu by pointing to the control menu with the mouse and clicking the left mouse button.

2. Choose MiNimize by clicking **Minimize** with the left mouse button. If the window occupied the entire screen, the window is reduced to occupy only a portion of the screen. If the window occupied only a portion of the screen, it is reduced to an icon.

   or

   Point to the minimize button in the upper-right corner of the window and click the left mouse button. The minimize button is the arrow pointing down.

Note

Use minimize to change the size of a window, even reducing the window to an icon. When a Windows

application is minimized, it continues processing. A
non-Windows application will continue processing if
Windows is in 386-Enhanced mode. Otherwise, the non-
Windows application will halt processing until it is
restored or maximized.

Mouse Customization

Control Panel

Purpose

Changes the sensitivity of the mouse, and enables you to
swap the mouse buttons.

Procedure

1. Choose Mouse Tracking Speed by clicking the
   Mouse Tracking Speed scroll box, pressing and
   holding the left mouse button, and dragging the
   scroll box to the desired setting. Release the mouse
   button. Move the mouse to check the tracking
   speed. If the speed is not yet correct, repeat this
   step.

2. Choose Double Click Speed by clicking the Double
   Click Speed scroll box, pressing and holding the
   left mouse button, and dragging the scroll box to
   the desired setting. Release the mouse button. Point
   to the Test button and double-click the left mouse
   button at different speeds. If the speed is not yet
   correct, repeat this step.

3. Choose Swap Left/Right Buttons to swap the
   mouse buttons. When the box is checked, the
   buttons are swapped.

4. Choose OK to accept the changes to the mouse by
   pressing Enter or by clicking the OK with the left
   mouse button.

   To abandon the merge, press Esc or click the
   Cancel with the left mouse button.

Notes

Mouse sensitivity combines two settings. The first setting is the mouse tracking speed. If the mouse tracking speed is set fast, you need little space on the Desktop to move the mouse. However, you trade accuracy with the mouse for the small desk space for movement. The second setting is double-click speed. The faster this setting, the more rapid you must double click the left mouse button.

You also can choose to swap the left and right mouse buttons. If you are left-handed, you can swap the mouse buttons so that the mouse button referred to as the left mouse button can be operated with your left index finger. To change this setting, start the Control Panel and choose the Settings Mouse command.

Move Files

File Manager

Purpose

Enables you to copy a file from one drive and directory to another drive and directory, deleting the original file.

Procedures

To move a file from one drive to another drive using the mouse

1. Start the File Manager.

2. Place the source disk and destination disk in the correct drives. For example, place the source disk in drive A and the destination disk in drive B.

3. Activate the source disk by pointing to the drive icon with the mouse and clicking the left mouse button.

4. Double-click the drive folder icon to display the files. If the drive has subdirectories, and you want

to copy the files from a subdirectory, then open the subdirectory by pointing to it and double-clicking the left mouse button.

5. Activate the Directory Tree window by pointing to the window and clicking the left mouse button.

6. Activate the destination drive by pointing to the correct drive icon and clicking the left mouse button.

7. Activate the source drive/directory window again.

8. Begin selecting the file or files to copy (see *Selecting Files*).

9. Point to the file icon of one of the selected files, and press and hold the **Alt** key, then press and hold the left mouse button.

10. Drag the Files icon to the destination drive or directory icon. When the Files icon is positioned on the correct destination drive or directory icon, release the mouse button, and release the **Alt** key.

The Moving dialog box appears on-screen. As the move progresses, you can click **Cancel** to abandon the move.

If you are performing a move to a diskette, ignore Steps 5 through 7. During Step 10, drag the files icon to the disk drive icon and release the mouse button, then release the **Alt** key.

To move a file from one drive to another drive using the keyboard.

1. Start the File Manager.

2. Place the source disk and destination disk in the correct drives. For example, place the source disk in drive A and the destination disk in drive B. If you are moving to or from a hard disk to a diskette, you only need to place the diskette in the drive.

3. Activate the source disk by pressing **Ctrl** and the letter associated with the drive. For example, press **Ctrl-A** to activate drive A.

4. Open the window that contains the files on the disk by selecting the drive folder icon and pressing **Enter**. If the drive has subdirectories, and you want to copy the files from a subdirectory, open the subdirectory by selecting it with the **up-** and **down-arrow** keys and pressing **Enter**.

5. Begin selecting the file or files to move (see *Selecting Files*).

6. Choose the **F**ile menu.

7. Choose **M**ove.

8. When the Move dialog box appears, type the name of the drive to which you want to copy. If you are copying to a disk in drive A, type **A:**.

9. Select **M**ove by pressing **Alt-M**.

   To abandon the move process, press **Esc**.

Notes

Be careful when you move a file. If you move a file to a drive or directory that contains a file by the same name, you may overwrite the original file with the file that you are moving, possibly losing data.

Moving Program Items

Program Manager

Purpose

Moves a program item to a different program group.

To move a program item using the menus

1. Start the Program Manager.

2. Open the program group that contains the program item you want to move. Select the **W**indow menu by pressing **Alt-W**, and then press the number associated with the program group.

or

Point to the program group and double-click the left mouse button.

3. Select the program item by using the **left-** and **right-arrow** keys, or by clicking the program item with the left mouse button.

4. Choose the File menu.

5. Choose Move. The Copy Program Item dialog box appears on-screen.

6. Choose To Group by pressing **Alt-T**, or clicking the **To Group** field with the left mouse button.

7. Select the correct program group by pressing the **up-** and **down-arrow** keys, or by clicking the drop-down list box, and then clicking the correct program group.

8. To complete the move, press **Enter** or click **OK** with the left mouse button. Press **Esc** or click **Cancel** with the left mouse button to abandon the move.

To copy a program item using the drag method (mouse only)

1. Start the Program Manager.

2. Open the program group that contains the program item you want to copy by pointing to the program group and double-clicking the left mouse button.

3. Point to the program item to copy, press and hold the left mouse button.

4. Drag the program item to the correct program group, then release the mouse button.

Note

When you move Program Items, make sure that the destination program group does not already contain a program item by the same name.

Moving Windows

General

Purpose

Enables you to move each open window so that each window is accessible.

Procedures

To move a window using the keyboard

1. Select the window you want to move by pressing **Ctrl-Esc** to call the Task List. Use the **up-** and **down-arrow** keys to select the correct window, and press **Enter**.

2. Choose the Control menu by pressing **Alt**, then the **space bar**.

3. Choose Move by pressing **M**.

4. Use the arrow keys to move the window on the screen. When the window is in the desired position, press **Enter**. Press **Esc** rather than Enter to return the window to its beginning position.

To move a window using the mouse

1. Point to the window you want to move and click the left mouse button.

2. Point to the window's title bar, press and hold the left mouse button.

3. Move the mouse, and the window moves. When the window is in the desired location, release the mouse button.

Pause a Print Job

Print Manager

Purpose

Pauses a print job. When you are ready, you can resume printing.

Procedure

1. Open the Print Manger window if it is not open. Use the Task List or double-click the **Print Manger** icon.

2. Select the printer you want to pause by using the arrow keys, or by pointing to the printer and clicking the left mouse button.

3. Choose the Pause button by pressing **Alt-P**, or by clicking the **Pause** button with the left mouse button. The printer pauses printing, and a hand appears before the printer name.

Note

Windows slices the computer's time among different processes to perform multiple tasks. Printing is one of the tasks. While Windows is printing in the background, you can work with applications in the foreground. If you are working with an application, and need maximum processing speed, pause the current print job so that Windows allocates more time to the application. Remember that Windows has not cancelled the print job, printing can be resumed.

Port Selection

Control Panel

Purpose

Assigns each printer to each port when you have several printers attached to a computer.

Procedure

1. Choose Installed Printers by pressing **Alt-P**, and use the arrow keys to select the correct printer.

   or

   Point to the correct printer and click the left mouse button.

2. Choose Configure by pressing **Alt-C**, or by clicking **Configure** with the left mouse button. The Printers-Configure dialog box appears on-screen.

3. Choose Ports by pressing **Alt-P**, and use the arrow keys to select the port to which the printer is attached.

   If you are using a mouse, point the mouse to the correct port, and click the left mouse button.

4. Choose OK by pressing **Enter**, or by clicking **OK** with the left mouse button.

   To abandon the selection, press **Esc** or click **Cancel** with the left mouse button. You return to the Printers dialog box.

5. From the Printers dialog box, choose OK by pressing **Enter** or by clicking **OK** with the left mouse button.

   To abandon the selection, press **Esc** or click **Cancel** with the left mouse button.

Notes

Because Windows permits you to assign a printer to a port that does not exist, you must make sure that ports you select actually exist on your computer, and that the printer you assigned is actually attached to the port.

Before you use this option, you must start the Control Panel. From the Control Panel, issue the Settings Printers command.

Print Files

File Manager

Purpose

Prints files rather than starting the application, loading the file, then issuing the print command.

Procedure

1. Start the File Manager.

2. Select the drive that contains the file you want to print by pressing **Ctrl** and the letter corresponding to the drive. For example, press **Ctrl-C** to select drive C.

   If you are using a mouse, point to the drive icon with the mouse and click the left mouse button.

3. Choose the directory (if one exists) that contains the file you want to print. Use the arrow keys to select the directory and press **Enter**, or click the subdirectory icon with the mouse and double-click the left mouse button.

4. Select the file to print using the arrow keys or by pointing to the file with the mouse and clicking the left mouse button.

   If you are using the mouse, and do not see the file, you may have to use the scroll bars.

5. Choose the File menu by pressing **Alt-F**, or by clicking the **File** menu with the left mouse button.

6. Choose the Print option by pressing **P**, or by clicking **Print** with the left mouse button.

7. The Print dialog box appears, and the file name that you chose is in the Print field. If the file name is correct, choose OK by pressing **Enter** or by clicking **OK** with the left mouse button.

   To abandon printing, press **Esc** or click **Cancel** with the left mouse button. The file will be sent to the Print Manager for printing to the current printer.

Print Priorities

Print Manager

Purpose

Determines how quickly you need a printed document. Switch between low, medium, and high priority.

Procedures

To set low priority

1. Bring the Print Manager to the foreground.

2. Choose the Options menu by pressing Alt-O, or by clicking **Options** with the left mouse button. A check mark appears next to Low Priority when it is selected.

3. Choose Low Priority by pressing L, or by clicking **Low Priority** with the left mouse button.

To set medium priority

1. Bring the Print Manager to the foreground.

2. Choose the Options menu by pressing Alt-O, or by clicking **Options** with the left mouse button. A check mark appears next to Medium Priority when it is selected.

3. Choose Medium Priority by pressing M, or by clicking **Medium Priority** with the left mouse button.

To set high priority

1. Bring the Print Manager to the foreground.

2. Choose the Options menu by pressing Alt-O, or by clicking **Options** with the left mouse button. A check mark appears next to High Priority when it is selected.

3. Choose High Priority by pressing H, or by clicking **High Priority** with the left mouse button.

Notes

Normally, the Print Manager is set to Medium priority. This setting is adequate because the printer normally can continue printing at a suitable speed in the background as you work with another application in the foreground.

For times when you need greater processing speed for the application in the foreground, set printing priority to low. If you need the document printed quickly, however, set the printing priority to high.

Printer Configuration

Control Panel

Purpose

Tells Windows about your printer. You specify paper size, what port it is attached to, what fonts it supports, and other features of the printer.

Procedures

To configure an Epson printer

1. Choose Installed Printers by pressing Alt-P, then using the arrow keys, select the printer to configure. If you are using a mouse, point to the Epson printer to configure under Installed Printers and click the left mouse button.

2. Choose Configure by pressing Alt-C, or by clicking the Configure button with the left mouse button.

3. Choose a port by pressing Alt-P. Then use the arrow keys to select the correct port.

   If you are using a mouse, point to the correct port under Ports and click the left mouse button.

4. Choose Device Not Selected by pressing Alt-D, or by clicking the Device Not Selected field with the left mouse button. Type the number of seconds that Windows should wait if a device is not attached or offline before an error message is displayed. The default number is 15, which should be adequate.

5. Choose Transmission Retry by pressing Alt-T, or by clicking the Transmission Retry field with the left mouse button. Type the number of seconds that Windows should wait before it displays a message that the device is not receiving characters.

6. Choose Setup by pressing Alt-S, or by clicking Setup with the left mouse button.

7. Choose PRinter by pressing Alt-R, or by clicking the Printer field with the left mouse button.

8. Choose the correct printer name by using the **up-** and **down-arrow** keys.

   If you are using a mouse, point to the correct printer name and click the left mouse button. Drag the scroll bar to view more printers if necessary.

9. Choose the type of Paper feed. Normally, you will use Tractor feed. If so, select Tractor by pressing **Alt-T**, or by clicking **Tractor** with the left mouse button.

10. Choose the Paper Width by pressing **Alt-W**. Then use the **up-** and **down-arrow** keys, select the correct width.

    If you are using a mouse, point to the correct **Paper width** and click the left mouse button. Use the scroll box if the correct width is not displayed.

11. Choose Paper Height by pressing **Alt-H**. Then use the **up-** and **down-arrow** keys, select the correct height.

    If you are using a mouse, point to the correct **Paper height** and click the left mouse button. Use the scroll box if the correct width is not displayed.

12. Select the correct Orientation. Select to print Portrait or Landscape by pressing **Alt-P** or **Alt-L**.

    If you are using a mouse, point to Portrait or Landscape and click the left mouse button.

13. Select the Graphics Resolution. For 9-pin Epson printers, choose 240x144, 120x144, or 120x72 by pressing **Alt-4**, **Alt-0**, or **Alt-7** respectively. For 24-pin Epson printers, choose 360x180 best graphics, 180x180 best text, or 120x180 fastest by pressing **Alt-3**, **Alt-8**, or **Alt-A** respectively.

    If you are using a mouse, point to one of the Graphics Resolutions and click the left mouse button.

14. Select one or more of the Other LQ Fonts. Press **Alt-F**, use the **up-** and **down-arrow** keys to highlight each font, and press the **space bar**.

If you are using a mouse, point to the font you want
to select and click the left mouse button. If you are
configuring a 9-pin printer, you may select No page
break, instead of Other LQ Fonts.

15. Choose OK to complete configuring the printer by
    pressing **Enter**, or by clicking **OK** with the left
    mouse button.

    To abandon the configuration, press **Esc** or click
    Cancel with the left mouse button. You return to
    the Printers-Configure dialog box.

16. Choose OK to complete configuring the printer by
    pressing **Enter**, or by clicking **OK** with the left
    mouse button.

    To abandon the configuration, press **Esc** or click
    Cancel with the left mouse button. You return to
    the Printers dialog box.

17. To make the selected printer the Default Printer,
    press **Alt-D** or point to the printer in Installed
    Printers with the mouse and double-click the left
    mouse button.

18. Choose Use Print Manager if the device should
    receive information from Windows' Print Manager,
    or if the printer will receive information directly
    from the application. Choose Use Print Manager by
    pressing **Alt-U**, or by clicking Use Print Manager
    with the left mouse button.

19. You can change the status of any printer. Select
    Status by pressing **Alt-S**. Then use the **up-** and
    down-arrow keys to select Active or Inactive.

    If you are using a mouse, point to either Active or
    Inactive and click the left mouse button. At least
    one printer must be active, normally the printer
    attached to LPT1.

To Configure an HP LaserJet Series II and Series III

1. Choose Installed Printers by pressing **Alt-P**. Then
   use the arrow keys to select the printer to configure.

   If you are using a mouse, point to the Hewlet-
   Packard printer to configure under Installed Printers
   and click the left mouse button.

2. Choose Configure by pressing Alt-C, or by clicking Configure with the left mouse button.

3. Choose a port by pressing Alt-P. Then use the arrow keys to select the correct port.

   If you are using a mouse, point to the correct port under Ports and click the left mouse button.

4. Choose Device Not Selected by pressing Alt-D, or by clicking the Device Not Selected field with the left mouse button. Type the number of seconds that Windows should wait if a device is not attached or off line before an error message is displayed.
   The default time is 15, which should be adequate.

5. Choose Transmission Retry by pressing Alt-T, or by clicking the Transmission Retry field with the left mouse button. Type the number of seconds that Windows should wait before it displays a message that the device is not receiving characters.

6. Choose Setup by pressing Alt-S, or by clicking Setup with the left mouse button.

7. Choose Printer by pressing Alt-P, or by clicking the Printer field with the left mouse button. Choose the drop-down list button by pressing Alt-down arrow, or by pointing to the drop-down list button and clicking the left mouse button.

8. Choose the correct printer name by using the up- and down-arrow keys, and then press Alt-up arrow.

   If you are using a mouse, point to the correct printer name and click the left mouse button.

9. Choose Paper Source by pressing Alt-S, or by clicking the Paper Source field with the left mouse button. Choose the drop-down list button by pressing Alt-down arrow, or by clicking the drop-down list button with the left mouse button.

10. Choose the correct paper source (normally Upper Tray) by using the up- and down-arrow keys, and then press Alt-up arrow.

   If you are using a mouse, point to the correct paper

source and click the left mouse button.

11. Choose Paper SiZe by pressing **Alt-Z**, or by clicking the **Paper Size** field with the left mouse button. Choose the drop-down list button by pressing **Alt-down arrow**, or by clicking the drop-down list button with the left mouse button.

12. Choose the correct paper size (normally Letter 8 1/2 x 11 inch) by using the **up-** and **down-arrow** keys, and then press **Alt-up arrow**.

   If you are using a mouse, point to the correct paper size and click the left mouse button.

13. Choose Memory by pressing **Alt-M** or by clicking the **Memory field** with the left mouse button. Choose the drop-down list button by pressing **Alt-down arrow** or by clicking the drop-down list button with the left mouse button.

14. Choose the correct amount of memory by using the **up-** and **down-arrow** keys, and then press **Alt-up arrow**.

   If you are using a mouse, point to the correct amount of memory and click the left mouse button.

15. Select the correct paper orientation. Select to print PoRtrait or Landscape by pressing **Alt-R** or **Alt-L**, or by clicking the appropriate option with the left mouse button.

16. Select the Graphics Resolution at which you want to print. Choose 75 dots per inch, 150 dots per inch, or 300 dots per inch by pressing **Alt-7**, **Alt-1**, or **Alt- 3** respectively.

   If you are using a mouse, point to one of the Graphics Resolutions and click the left mouse button.

17. You can choose up to two CarTridges to plug into the printer. Using the keyboard, press **Alt-T**, and use the **up-** and **down-arrow** keys to highlight a cartridge. Press the **space bar** to select the cartridge. Repeat this procedure to select the second cartridge.

   If you are using a mouse, use the scroll bars to

display the cartridges. Point to the correct cartridge and click the left mouse button. Point to the second cartridge and click the left mouse button again.

18. Choose Copies by pressing Alt-C, or by clicking the Copies field with the left mouse button. Type the number of copies that should be printed each time you choose to print. Normally, this value will be 1, however, typing 2 here will save you from running to the copier if you normally copy all documents.

19. Choose OK to complete configuring the printer by pressing Enter, or by clicking OK with the left mouse button.

    To abandon the configuration, press Esc or click Cancel with the left mouse button. You return to the Printers-Configure dialog box.

20. Choose OK to complete configuring the printer by pressing Enter or by clicking OK with the left mouse button.

    To abandon the configuration, press Esc or click Cancel with the left mouse button. You return to the Printers dialog box.

21. To make the selected printer the Default Printer, press Alt-D, or point to the printer in Installed Printers and double-click the left mouse button.

22. Choose Use Print Manager if the device should receive information from Windows' Print Manager, or if the printer will receive information directly from the application. Choose Use Print Manager by pressing Alt-U, or by clicking Use Print Manager with the left mouse button.

23. You can change the status of any printer. by pressing Alt-S, and using the up- and down-arrow keys to select Active or Inactive.

    If you are using a mouse, point to either Active or Inactive and click the left mouse button. At least one printer must be active, normally the printer attached to LPT1.

To Configure a Postscript Printer

1. Choose Installed Printers by pressing **Alt-P**, then using the arrow keys to select the printer to configure.

   If you are using a mouse, point to the postscript printer to configure under Installed Printers and click the left mouse button.

2. Choose Configure by pressing **Alt-C**, or by clicking **Configure** with the left mouse button.

3. Choose a port to use from Ports by pressing **Alt-P**, then use the arrow keys to select the correct port.

   If you are using a mouse, point to the correct port under Ports and click the left mouse button.

4. Choose Device Not Selected by pressing **Alt-D** or by pointing to the Device Not Selected field with the mouse and clicking the left mouse button. Type the number of seconds that Windows should wait if a device is not not attached or off line before an error message is displayed. The default is 15, which should be adequate.

5. Choose Transmission Retry by pressing **Alt-T** or by pointing to the Transmission Retry field with the mouse and clicking the left mouse button. Type the number of seconds that Windows should wait before displaying a message that the device is not receiving characters.

6. Choose Setup by pressing **Alt-S**, or by clicking the Setup button with the left mouse button.

7. Choose Printer by pressing **Alt-P** or by pointing to the Printer field with the mouse and clicking the left mouse button. Choose the drop-down list button by pressing **Alt-down arrow**, or by pointing to the drop-down list button with the mouse and clicking the left mouse button.

8. Choose the correct printer name by using the **up-** and **down-arrow** keys, then press **Alt-up arrow**. If you are using a mouse, point to the correct printer name and click the left mouse button.

9. Choose Paper Source by pressing **Alt-S**, or by pointing to the Paper Source field with the mouse and clicking the left mouse button. Choose the drop-down list button by pressing **Alt-down arrow**, or by pointing to the drop-down list button with the mouse and clicking the left mouse button.

10. Choose the correct paper source (normally Upper Tray) by using the **up-** and **down-arrow** keys, then press **Alt-up arrow**. If you are using a mouse, point to the correct paper source and click the left mouse button.

11. Choose Paper SiZe by pressing **Alt-Z**, or by pointing to the **Paper Size** field with the mouse and clicking the left mouse button. Choose the drop-down list button by pressing **Alt-down arrow**, or by pointing to the drop-down list button with the mouse and clicking the left mouse button.

12. Choose the correct paper size (normally Letter 8 1/2 x 11 inch) by using the **up-** and **down-arrow** keys, then press **Alt-up arrow**. If you are using a mouse, point to the correct paper size and click the left mouse button.

13. Choose Scaling by pressing **Alt-N**, or by pointing to the **Scaling** field with the mouse and clicking the left mouse button.

14. Type the percent of scaling, normally 100.

15. Select the correct paper orientation. Select to print PoRtrait or Landscape by pressing **Alt-R** or **Alt-L**, or by pointing to PoRtrait or Landscape with the mouse and clicking the left mouse button.

16. Choose Copies by pressing **Alt-C** or by pointing to the **Copies** field with the mouse and clicking the left mouse button. Type the number of copies that should be printed each time you choose to print. Normally, this value will be 1, however, typing 2 here will save you from running to the copier if you normally copy all documents.

17. Choose Options by pressing **Alt-O** or by pointing to the **Options** button with the mouse and clicking the left mouse button. The Options dialog box appears.

18. Choose from the following, pressing **Alt** and the boldfaced letter to choose the option:

Option	*Meaning*
Print To **Printer**	Send output to printer.
En**C**apsulated PostScript File	Capture output in a file.
Job Timeout	Enter number of seconds Windows waits for the printer to respond before sending an error message to the screen.
Margins **Default**	Use the default margins.
None	Use no margins.
Header Down**L**oad each job.	Send a header to the printer each time you print.
Already downloaded	Do not send a header to the printer each time you print.

Choose OK by pressing **Enter,** or by clicking **OK** with the left mouse button to return to the previous dialog box.

19. Choose OK to complete configuring the printer by pressing **Enter**, or by clicking **OK** with the left mouse button.

To abandon the configuration, press **Esc** or click **Cancel** with the left mouse button.

You return to the Printers-Configure dialog box.

20. Choose OK to complete configuring the printer by pressing **Enter**, or by clicking **OK** with the left mouse button.

To abandon the configuration, press **Esc** or click **Cancel** with the left mouse button.

You return to the Printers dialog box.

21. To make the selected printer the Default Printer, press **Alt-D** or point to the printer in Installed Printers and double-click the left mouse button.

22. Choose Use Print Manager if the device should receive information from Windows' Print Manager or if the printer will receive information directly from the application. Choose Use Print Manager by pressing **Alt-U**, or by clicking Use **Print Manager** with the left mouse button.

23. You can change the status of any printer. Select Status by pressing **Alt-S**, then use the **up-** and **down-arrow** keys to select Active or Inactive.

    If you are using a mouse, point to either **Active** or **Inactive** and click the left mouse button. At least one printer must be active, normally the printer attached to LPT1.

Notes

Dot matrix printers are easy to configure. Windows needs to know a the size of paper, and the port to which the printer is attached.

Configuring a laser printer, and some ink printers is different. You must specify how much memory is installed in the printer, what fonts (cartridge and soft) that are available for the printer to use, whether you plan to print in portrait or landscape orientation, and. what resolution in Dots Per Inch (DPI) you plan to print graphics.

Before you configure your printer, you must start the Control Panel. From the Control Panel, issue the command Settings Printers.

Printing

Purpose

Enables you to print information from a file to the printer.

Procedure

1. Start the Notepad accessory.

2. Open the file you want to print with the File Open command.

3. Choose the File, Page SeTup command, and change any page settings for the printer you will use to print the file.

4. Choose the File, PRinter Setup command, and change any printer settings.

5. Choose the File menu by pressing Alt-F, or by clicking the File menu with the left mouse button.

6. Choose Print by pressing P, or by clicking Print with the left mouse button.

7. When the Notepad dialog box appears, you can abandon printing by pressing Esc or by clicking Cancel with the left mouse button.

Notes

Before printing, make sure that you have the correct printer selected. Select the printer with the File, PRinter Setup command.

Check File Page SeTup to make sure that you have the correct margins set for your printer.

Printing Appointments

Calendar

Purpose

Prints a list of appointments so that you may consult the
list even when you are away from your computer.

Procedure

1. Start the Calendar accessory.

2. Open the file you want to print with the File Open
   command.

3. Choose the File, Page SeTup command, and change
   any page settings for the printer to which you want
   to print.

4. Choose the File PRinter Setup command, and
   change any printer settings.

5. Choose the File menu by pressing Alt-F, or by
   clicking the File menu with the left mouse button.

6. Choose Print by pressing P, or by clicking Print
   with the left mouse button.

7. Choose From by pressing Alt-F, or by clicking the
   From field with the left mouse button. Type the
   beginning appointment day.

   For example, if the first day to print is June 26,
   1990, type 6/26/90.

8. Optionally, choose To by pressing Alt-T, or by
   clicking the To field with the left mouse button.
   Type the ending appointment day to print.

   For example, if the last day to print is June 28,
   1990, type 6/28/90.

9. To begin printing, choose OK by pressing **Enter** or by clicking **OK** with the left mouse button.

   To abandon printing, press **Esc** or click **Cancel** with the left mouse button.

10. When the Calendar dialog box appears, you may cancel printing by pressing **Esc** or by clicking **Cancel** with the left mouse button.

Notes

Before printing, make sure that you have the correct printer selected. Select the correct printer with the File, PRinter Setup command. Also, check File, Page SeTup to make sure that the correct margins are set for your printer.

Before printing, you must enter at least a beginning date. If you type a beginning date, but no ending date, then the appointments from the beginning date are printed. If no beginning date is typed, only an ending date is printed. If neither a beginning nor an ending date is typed, then you receive an error message telling you that you entered an invalid date range.

Printing Cards ═══════════════════

Cardfile

Purpose

Enables you to print the current card or all cards in a cardfile database.

Procedures

To print the current card

1. Start the Cardfile accessory.

2. Open the file from which to print a card using the File, Open command.

3. Search for the correct card to print using the Search, Go To or the Search, Find command.

4. Choose the File, Page SeTup command, and change any page settings for the printer to which you want to print.

5. Choose the File, PRinter Setup command and change any printer settings.

6. Choose the File menu by pressing **Alt-F**, or by clicking the **File** menu with the left mouse button.

7. Choose Print by pressing **P**, or by clicking **Print** with the left mouse button.

8. When the Cardfile dialog box appears, you may abandon printing by pressing **Esc** or by clicking **Cancel** with the left mouse button.

To print all cards

1. Start the Cardfile accessory.

2. Open the file from which to print a card using the File Open command.

3. Choose File Page SeTup, and change any page settings for the printer to which you will print.

4. Choose the File PRinter Setup command, and change any printer settings.

5. Choose the File menu by pressing **Alt-F**, or by clicking the **File** menu with the left mouse button.

6. Choose Print ALl by pressing **L**, or by clicking **Print All** with the left mouse button.

7. When the Cardfile dialog box appears, you may abandon printing by pressing **Esc** or by clicking **Cancel** with the left mouse button.

Notes

Before printing, make sure that you have the correct printer selected. Select the correct printer with the File, PRinter Setup command. Also, check File, Page SeTup to make sure that the correct margins are set for your printer.

If you are printing just one card, make sure that the current card is the correct card to print.

Program Properties

Program Manager

Purpose

Contains the Program Item name, file name, and location on the disk. The Program Properties also contain a picture of the icon.

Procedure

To change a program's properties

1. Start the File Manager.

2. Open the Program Group that contains the Program Item whose properties you want to change. Choose the Window menu, and then choose the number associated with the Program Group.

3. Select the Program Item for which you want to change the properties by using the arrow keys, or by pointing to the Program Item and clicking the left mouse button.

4. Choose the File menu by pressing Alt-F, or by clicking the File menu with the left mouse button.

5. Choose the Properties option by pressing P, or by clicking the Properties option with the left mouse button.

   The Program Item Properties dialog box appears on-screen.

6. Select Description by pressing Alt-D, or by clicking the Description field with the left mouse button.

7. Type the description that you want to appear under the Program Item icon.

8. Select Command Line by pressing Alt-C, or by clicking the Command Line field with the left mouse button.

9. Type the drive, directory, and full file name of the file that will start the Program Item.

For example, if EXCEL.EXE is the name that starts the Excel application, and the file resides in C:\EXCEL, type

C:\EXCEL\EXCEL.EXE.

If you are not sure of the program name or location, choose the **B**rowse button so that you can look on the disk and select the correct program name.

10. To change the icon, choose the Change **I**con button. Press **Alt-I** or click the **Change Icon** button with the left mouse button.

    The Select Icon dialog box appears on-screen.

11. Choose the View **N**ext button to see the next icon, the OK button to choose the current icon, or the Cancel button to abandon selecting the icon.

12. Choose OK by pressing **Enter** or by clicking **OK** with the left mouse button to save the changes to the Program Item Properties.

    To abandon changes, press **Esc** or click **Cancel** with the left mouse button.

Note

Before you change the properties of a Program Item, you may want to note the original properties.

Record a Macro

Recorder

Purpose

Records keystrokes and mouse movements that you use repeatedly. You can save these macros for recall at a later time.

Procedures

To record a macro

1. Start the Recorder accessory.

2. If you are adding the macro to an existing macro file, use the **F**ile **O**pen command to open the macro file.

3. Choose the **M**acro menu by pressing **Alt-M**, or by clicking the **Macro** menu with the left mouse button.

4. Choose the Re**C**ord option by pressing **C**, or by clicking **Record** with the left mouse button.

   The Record Macro dialog box appears on-screen.

5. Choose Record Macro **N**ame by pressing **Alt-N**, or by clicking the **Record Macro Name** field with the left mouse button. Type the name of the macro to record.

6. Choose a Shortcut **K**ey by pressing **Alt-K**, or by pressing **Alt-down arrow** to choose the drop-down list box.

   If you are using a mouse, click the **Shortcut Key** drop-down list box with the left mouse button.

7. Select the key to use with the arrow keys, and then press **Alt-up arrow**.

   If you are using a mouse, point to the character and press the left mouse button.

8. Use the **Tab** key and the **space bar** to choose Ctrl, Shift, or Alt. When an X marks one of these keys, that key must be used in conjunction with the Shortcut Key to activate the macro.

   For example, if Ctrl and Shift both contain X's, and the shortcut key is F10, you must press and hold **Ctrl** and **Shift**, press **F10**, and then release all keys to start the macro.

9. Choose **P**layback to specify how the macro should play back when activated.

10. With the To field active, press **Alt-down arrow**, or point to the drop-down list box. Choose one of the following:

Option	*Meaning*
Any Application	Replays in any application.

Same Application   Replays only in the application
                     that the macro was recorded.

Use the arrow keys to select an option, then press
Alt-up arrow, or point to the option with the
mouse and click the left mouse button.

11. Press **Tab** to choose the Speed field, or click the
    Speed field with the left mouse button.

12. With the Speed field active, press **Alt-down arrow**,
    or point to the drop-down list box for Speed.
    Choose one of the following:

Option	*Meaning*
Fast	Replays as quickly as Windows will allow.
Recorded Speed	Replays only at the speed at which it was recorded.

Use the arrow keys to select an option, then press
Alt-up arrow, or point to the option with the
mouse and click the left mouse button.

13. Press **Tab**, then use the space bar to toggle whether
    the macro should play in a continuous loop, or
    whether the macro should play only once. If you are
    using a mouse, point to the **Continuous Loop** box
    and click the left mouse button.

14. Choose Record **M**ouse by pressing **Alt-M**, or by
    clicking the **Record Mouse** field with the left
    mouse button.

15. Choose the Record **M**ouse drop-down list box by
    pressing **Alt-down arrow**, or by clicking the
    Record Mouse drop-down list box with the left
    mouse button. Choose one of the following:

Option	*Meaning*
Ignore Mouse	Records keystrokes only.
Everything	Records keystrokes, mouse movements, and mouse selections.

Clicks + Drags   Records mouse movements and
                     selections only.

Use the arrow keys to select an option, and press
Alt-up arrow, or point to the option with the
mouse and click the left mouse button.

16. Choose **R**elative to by pressing **Alt-R**, or by
    clicking the **Relative to** field with the left mouse
    button.

17. Choose the **R**elative to drop-down list box by
    pressing **Alt-down arrow**, or by clicking the
    Relative to drop-down list box with the left mouse
    button. Choose one of the following options:

Option	*Meaning*
Screen	All recorded mouse movements and selections are relative to the entire screen.
Window	All recorded mouse movements and selections are relative to a window.

Use the arrow keys to select an option, then press
Alt-up arrow, or point to the option with the
mouse and click the left mouse button.

18. Choose **D**escription by pressing **Alt-D**, or by
    clicking the **Description** field with the left mouse
    button. Type a description of the macro.

19. Choose **S**tart by pressing **Alt-S**, or by clicking **Start**
    with the left mouse button. You can start recording
    a macro in the application that was active prior to
    activating the Recorder accessory.

To stop recording or pause and resume a macro

1. Press **Ctrl-Break** or click the **Recorder** icon with
   the left mouse button.

   The Recorder dialog box appears on-screen.

2. Select one of the following options:

Option	Meaning
Save Macro	Stops recording the macro and keeps all keystrokes and mouse movements.
Resume Recording	Continues recording keystrokes. The macro is not complete.
Cancel Recording	Stops recording the macro and forgets all keystrokes and mouse movements.

3. Choose OK by pressing **Enter** or by clicking **OK** with the left mouse button.

To save a macro file

1. Start and stop recording a macro according to the preceding instructions.

2. Choose the File menu by pressing **Alt-F**, or by clicking the **File** menu with the left mouse button.

3. Choose Save **As** if you are saving a new file or Save if you are resaving a file. If you choose Save As, then type a file name and choose OK by pressing **Enter** or by clicking **OK** with the left mouse button.

Notes

When you record a macro, you can choose from many options. For example, you can select to record only keystrokes or keystrokes and mouse movements. If you record mouse movements, you can specify that the movements should relate only to a window or to the entire screen.

Besides giving each macro a name, you may also assign the macro a key combination. For example, assign Ctrl-F10 so that when you press **Ctrl-F10**, the macro automatically starts.

When you record a macro, make sure that you do not try to use the same name or key combinations for two different macros.

Rename Files

File Manager

Purpose

Enables you to assign a new filename.

To rename a file

1. Start the File Manager.

2. From the File Manager, select the drive containing the file or files you want to rename by pressing **Ctrl** and the letter of the drive. For example, press **Ctrl-C** for drive C.

   If you are using a mouse, point to the disk drive icon with the mouse and click the left mouse button.

3. From the Directory Tree, open the subdirectory that contains the file or files you want renamed. Use the arrow keys to select the subdirectory and press **Enter**, or point to the subdirectory and click the left mouse button.

   If the subdirectory window that opens contains additional subdirectories that need to be opened, repeat this step.

4. Select the file to rename (see *Selecting Files*).

5. Choose the **F**ile menu by pressing **Alt-F**, or by clicking the **File** menu with the left mouse button.

6. Choose Re**N**ame by pressing **N**, or by clicking **Rename** with the left mouse button.

7. When the Rename dialog box appears, type the new name in the **T**o field.

8. Choose **R**ename by pressing **Enter**, or by clicking **Rename** with the left mouse button. To abandon Rename file, choose Cancel by pressing **Esc** or by clicking **Cancel** with the left mouse button.

Note

When you rename a file, you cannot use a name that already exists.

Restore Windows

General

Purpose

Changes an icon or a window to the size it was previously.

Procedures

To restore a window from an icon

1. Select the icon to restore by pressing Alt-Esc, or by pointing to the icon with the mouse and clicking the left mouse button.

2. If you selected the icon using the keyboard, then press Alt-space bar to choose the control menu. If you selected the icon using the mouse, the Control menu is already open.

3. Choose Restore by pressing R, or by clicking Restore with the left mouse button.

To restore a window to its previous size

1. Select the window to restore by pressing Alt-Esc, or by pointing to the window with the mouse and clicking the left mouse button.

2. Choose the Control menu by pressing Alt-space bar, or by clicking the Control menu with the left mouse button.

3. Choose Restore by pressing R, or by clicking Restore with the left mouse button.

Note

> Restore is used as an "automatic minimize/maximize" in that it minimizes a previously maximized window, and maximizes a previously minimized window or icon.

═|Resume a Print Job|════════

Print Manager

Purpose

> Resumes a print job that has been paused.

Procedure

1. Open the Print Manger window if it is not open by using the Task List or by double-clicking the **Print Manger** icon with the left mouse button.

2. Select the printer you want to resume printing by using the arrow keys or by pointing to the printer with the mouse and clicking the left mouse button.

3. Choose the **R**esume button by pressing **Alt-R**, or by clicking **Resume** with the left mouse button. The printer will resume printing, and the hand that appeared before the printer name disappears.

Notes

> Windows slices the computer's time among different processes to perform multiple tasks. Printing is one of the tasks. As Windows prints in the background, you can work with applications in the foreground.
>
> If you are working with an application, and need maximum processing speed, you can pause the current print job so that Windows allocates more time to the application. When you are ready, you may resume printing.

Run Files

File Manager

Purpose

Enables you to start applications from the File Manager.

Procedure

1. Start the File Manager.

2. Choose Run by pressing R, or by clicking Run with the left mouse button.

3. When the Run dialog box appears, type the program to run in the Command Line field.

   Select Run Minimized if the application should shrink to an icon.

8. Choose OK by pressing Enter or by clicking OK with the left mouse button.

   To abandon Run, choose Cancel by pressing Esc or by clicking Cancel with the left mouse button.

Note

You may have an application or a utility that you use so rarely that you do not want to create a Program Item for it. You may start the application or utility from the File Manager instead.

Search for Files

File Manager

Purpose

Enables you to find a file when you do not remember in what directory the file is located.

Procedure

1. Start the File Manager application.

2. Choose the File menu by pressing Alt-F, or by clicking the File menu with the left mouse button.

3. Choose SearcH by pressing H, or by clicking Search with the left mouse button.

   The Search dialog box appears on-screen.

4. Choose Search For by pressing Alt-F, or by clicking the Search For field with the left mouse button.

5. Type the search string, using wild card characters if desired.

   Suppose, for example, that you are seaching for LETTER.TXT. Type LETTER.TXT. If you are searching for all files with the NTE extension, then type *.NTE.

6. Choose Search Entire Disk by pressing Alt-E, or by clicking the Search Entire Disk box with the left mouse button to toggle whether to search the entire disk drive or to search the directory branch only.

7. To begin searching, choose OK by pressing Enter or by clicking OK with the left mouse button.

   To abandon the search, press Esc or click Cancel with the left mouse button.

8. If files are found, the Search Results window appears. You may act upon the files shown, such as activating them, copying them, and deleting them.

Notes

When searching for files, you may search through a directory branch or search through the entire disk.

All files that are found are displayed in a window with the entire path pointing to the file. You can open any of the files in the window, starting an associated application.

Searching for Cards

Cardfile

Purpose

Finds a desired card in the cardfile.

Procedures

To search for a card using the index line

1. Start the Cardfile accessory.

2. Open the cardfile using the File Open command.

3. Choose the Search menu by pressing **Alt-S**, or by clicking the **Search** menu with the left mouse button.

4. Choose Go To by pressing **G**, or by clicking **Go To** with the left mouse button. The Go To dialog box appears on-screen.

5. Type the text that you want to search on the index line.

6. To begin searching, choose OK by pressing **Enter** or by clicking **OK** with the left mouse button.

   To abandon the search, press **Esc** or click **Cancel** with the left mouse button. If the card is found, it appears on the top of the card stack.

To search for a card using Find

1. Start the Cardfile accessory.

2. Open the cardfile using the File, Open command.

3. Choose the Search menu by pressing **Alt-S**, or by clicking the **Search** menu with the left mouse button.

4. Choose Find by pressing **F**, or by clicking **Find** with the left mouse button. The Find dialog box appears on-screen.

5. Type the text for which you want to search.

6. To begin searching, choose OK by pressing Enter
or by clicking OK with the left mouse button.

To abandon the search, press Esc or click Cancel
with the left mouse button. If the card is found, it
appears on the top of the card stack.

To search for the next card using Find Next

1. Choose the Search menu by pressing Alt-S, or by
clicking the Search menu with the left mouse
button.

2. Choose Find Next by pressing N, or by clicking
Find Next with the left mouse button.

The Find dialog box appears on-screen.

Note

You can search for a card in two ways. One way is to
use Go To a card. This method enables you quickly to
find a card based on information in the card's index line.
The second way is to use Find a card. Find is not as
quick as Go To. Find searches for information on a card
in any location other than in the index line.

Searching for Text

Notepad

Purpose

Looks for text in a document or file.

Procedures

To search for text using Find

1. Start the Notepad accessory.

2. Open the Notepad file using the File, Open
command.

3. Choose the Search menu by pressing **Alt-S**, or by clicking the **Search** menu with the left mouse button.

4. Choose Find by pressing **F**, or by clicking **Find** with the left mouse button. The Find dialog box appears on-screen.

5. Choose Find What by pressing **Alt-F**, or by clicking the **Find What** field with the left mouse button.

6. Type the text to find.

7. Choose Match Upper/Lowercase by pressing **Alt-M**, or by clicking the **Match Upper/Lowercase** box with the left mouse button. This option is a toggle.

8. Select either FOrward or Backward by pressing **Alt-O** or **Alt-B.** If you are using a mouse, click **Forward** or **Backward** with the left mouse button.

9. To choose OK, press **Enter** or click **OK** with the left mouse button.

   To abandon the find, press **Esc** or click **Cancel** with the left mouse button.

To search for the next occurrence using Find Next

1. Choose the Search menu by pressing **Alt-S**, or by clicking the **Search** menu with the left mouse button.

2. Choose Find Next by pressing **N**, or by clicking **Find Next** with the left mouse button. The Find dialog box appears on-screen.

Notes

When searching for text with the Notepad, you can specify to make the search case sensitive. You also can search forward through the file, or backward through the file.

Searching always originates from the position of the cursor.

Selecting Files

File Manager

Purpose

Highlights a file or group of files to act upon.

Procedures

To select a single file using the keyboard

1. Start the File Manager.

2. From the Directory Tree, select and open the directory that contains the file you want to act on. Use the arrow keys to select the correct directory and press **Enter**, or issue the **F**ile **O**pen command.

3. Highlight the correct file using the arrow keys.

To select a single file using the mouse

1. Start the File Manager.

2. From the Directory Tree, point to the directory that contains the file or files to select and double-click the left mouse button.

3. Point to the correct file and click the mouse button to select the file

To select a contiguous group of files using the keyboard

1. Start the File Manager.

2. From the Directory Tree, select and open the directory that contains the file to select. Use the arrow keys to select the correct directory and press **Enter** or issue the **F**ile, **O**pen command.

3. Highlight the first file using the arrow keys.

4. Press and hold the **Shift** key, then use the arrow keys to begin highlighting files.

   The highlight begins expanding over the files. Use the **up-** and **down-arrow** keys to highlight the next or previous file in a column, or the **right-** and **left-arrow** keys to highlight columns of files. When all necessary files have been selected, release the keys.

To select a contiguous group of files using the mouse

1. Start the File Manager.

2. From the Directory Tree, point to the directory that contains the file or files to select and double-click the left mouse button.

3. Point to the first file to select and click the mouse button to select the file.

4. Point to the last file to select, press and hold the Shift key, then click the left mouse button. Release the shift key.

To select a non-contiguous group of files using the keyboard

1. Start the File Manager.

2. From the Directory Tree, select and open the directory that contains the file to select. Use the arrow keys to select the correct directory and press Enter or issue the File, Open command.

3. Highlight the first file using the arrow keys.

4. Press Shift-F8. The selection outline begins blinking.

5. Using the arrow keys, move the selection outline to the next file to select. Press the space bar. Repeat this step to continue selecting files.

To select a non-contiguous group of files using the mouse

1. Start the File Manager.

2. From the Directory Tree, point to the directory that contains the file or files to select and double-click the left mouse button.

3. Point to the first file to select and click the mouse button to select the file.

4. Point to the next file to select, press and hold the Ctrl key, then click the left mouse button. Release the Ctrl key. Repeat this step to continue selecting files.

Note

You can select a single file, group of files, or files that are not in a group. You can copy, delete, or perform other operations on the files you select.

Sizing Windows

General

Purpose

Changes the size of a window.

Procedures

To size a window using the keyboard

1. Activate the window to size using the Task List.

2. Press **Alt-space bar** to activate the window's Control Menu.

3. Choose Size by pressing S.

4. Press the arrow key that points to the side of the window to begin sizing. Pressing the up arrow begins sizing the top of the window. The right arrow begins sizing the right side of the window. The left arrow begins sizing the left side of the window. The down arrow begins sizing the bottom side of the window.

5. As an option, after you have selected the side to begin sizing, you then may select a corner to begin sizing. After pressing the up arrow or the down arrow, pressing the right or left arrow enables you to begin sizing the right or left corner of the side you selected. If you originally pressed the right or left arrow key to begin sizing the right or left side of the window, pressing the up or down arrow key enables you to begin sizing the top or bottom corner of the respective side.

6. Use the arrow keys to change the size of the window. You will see the outline of the window change to show you the size of the window.

7. Press **Enter** to quit sizing the window.

To size a window using the mouse

1. Activate the window to size by pointing to it with the mouse and clicking the left mouse button. If the window you want is hidden by another window, either move the window or access the Task List.

2. Move the mouse to point to the side or corner to begin sizing. If you point to a side of the window, the mouse arrow on the screen will change to a double-headed arrow that points left and right or up and down. If you point to a corner of the window, the mouse arrow will change to a double-headed arrow that points diagonally.

3. When the arrow has changed to a double-headed arrow, press and hold the left mouse button.

4. Move the mouse. You will see the outline of the window change to show you the size of the window. When the window is the desired size, release the mouse button.

Note

Windows can be changed in size. You will find this helpful especially when you have several windows open at once. Normally, when you are working with an application, you will want the foreground application to take up the entire screen, or at least most of the screen. However, if you are copying information from one window to another, or if you must monitor activity in one window while you work in another, then you will want to size each window so that both are visible.

Sound Toggle

Control Panel

Purpose

Toggles the warning beep.

Procedure

1. Start the Control Panel.

2. Choose Sound by issuing the command **S**ettings **S**ound, or by pointing to the **Sound** icon with the mouse and double-clicking the left mouse button.

3. Toggle **W**arning Beep by pressing **W**, or by clicking the **Warning Beep** box with the left mouse button. When the **W**arning Beep box is marked, then a beep sounds.

4. To choose OK, press **Enter** or click **OK** with the left mouse button.

   To abandon the change to **W**arning Beep, press **Esc** or click **Cancel** with the left mouse button.

Note

When Windows warns you of an error, it not only warns you with a message in a dialog box, but it also sounds a beep. If the beep annoys you, or if you work in an area where sound of more than keyboard clicking distracts others, you can shut off the beep. Because sound is a toggle, you can turn the beep on and off with the same steps.

Special Appointments

Calendar

Purpose

Enters a time in the Calendar accessory other than the default times.

Procedures

To insert a special appointment time

1. Start the Calendar Accessory.

2. Select the correct day for the special appointment.

3. Choose the **O**ptions menu by pressing **Alt-O**, or by clicking **Options** with the left mouse button.

4. Choose Special Time by pressing **S**, or by clicking **Special Time** with the left mouse button.

   The Special Time dialog box appears on-screen.

5. Choose Special Time by pressing **Alt-S**, or by clicking the **Special Time** field with the left mouse button.

6. Type the special time to insert according to the twelve hour clock.

   To enter 1:15 PM, type **1:15**.

7. Select **AM** or **PM** by pressing **Alt-A** or **Alt-P**, respectively.

   If you are using a mouse, click **AM** or **PM** with the left mouse button.

8. To Insert the special time, press **Alt-I**, or click **Insert** with the left mouse button.

   The special time is inserted in the day, and the cursor is positioned in the special time memo field so that you can enter a message for the special time.

To remove a special appointment time

1. Start the Calendar Accessory.

2. Select the day that contains the special appointment to remove.

3. Choose the Options menu by pressing **Alt-O**, or by clicking **Options** with the left mouse button.

4. Choose Special Time by pressing **S**, or by clicking **Special Time** with the left mouse button.

   The Special Time dialog box appears on-screen.

5. Choose Special Time by pressing **Alt-S**, or by clicking the **Special Time** field with the left mouse button.

6. Type the special time to delete according to the twelve hour clock.

   To delete 1:15 PM, type **1:15**.

7. Select **AM** or **PM** by pressing **Alt-A** or **Alt-P**, respectively.

If you are using a mouse, click **AM** or **PM** with the left mouse button.

8. To **D**elete the special time, press **Alt-D**, or click **Delete** with the left mouse button.

The special time is deleted.

Note

Often an appointment occurs on a time other than the hour. Suppose, for example, that you are a doctor who schedules appointments at 15-minute or half-hour increments. Even though the default appointment times in the Calendar accessory occur on the hour, you can create a special time for any time of the day, accurate to the minute.

Standard Mode

PIF Editor

Purpose

Allocates computer resources for the program to use. To use Standard DOS applications with Windows, you must create a Program Information File (PIF).

Procedures

To select the Standard mode using the keyboard or mouse

1. Start the **PIF Editor** accessory.

2. Select Mode.

3. If there is not a check mark next to Standard, then select Standard.

To enter information for the Standard Mode (using Lotus 1-2-3 Release 2.2 as an example)

1. Enter the Program Filename. You must enter the entire name used to start the program including the path, root name, and extension. An example is **C:\123\LOTUS.COM.**

2. Enter the Window Title that appears at the top of the window. Enter, for example, **Lotus Access System**.

3. Enter any **O**ptional Parameters. These parameters are used by the program when it starts, such as switches. Lotus 1-2-3 allows you to supply a different configuration, called a SET file. You can enter, for example, **COLOR.SET**, if this is the name of a valid configuration file.

4. Enter the **S**tart-up Directory that the program will use. Some programs store their data in the current directory. In this example, type **C:\123**.

5. Select the Correct **V**ideo Mode. If the program displays only text, select Text. If the program displays graphics only or text and graphics, select Graphics/Multiple Text.

6. Enter the memory required to run the program in the Memory Requirements: KB **R**equired field. If the minimum memory required to run the program is 256K, then type **256**.

7. Enter the XMS Memory (extended memory) requirements and limit. If the program uses XMS memory, enter the KB **R**equired. To prevent the program from using all XMS memory, enter the KB **LI**mit.

8. If the program controls one of the communications ports or the keyboard, then select COM**1**, COM**2**, COM**3**, COM**4**, or **K**eyboard.

9. To keep from exchanging data between this program and another, select No Screen **E**xchange. Selecting this option also frees some memory.

10. Select Prevent Program S**W**itch to keep this program from being switched away (and another program becoming the current program). This procedure is important for communications which must be active at all times.

11. Select **C**lose Window on Exit to close the window when you quit the program.

12. Select Reserve Shortcut Keys to enable the program to use the key combinations Alt+Tab, Alt+Esc, Ctrl+Esc, PrtSc or Alt+PrtSc. Normally, Windows uses these keys. If the program needs the keys, select each key combination the programs uses, and Windows will ignore it.

Note

If you have a computer based on the 80386 microprocessor, you can run several DOS applications at the same time. Windows must have more information about each application to multitask each application than it needs to run just a single DOS application. Selecting the 386 Enhanced Mode enables you to give Windows the needed information.

Starting Programs

Program Manager

Purpose

Activates applications in memory.

Procedures

To start an application using the keyboard

1. Open the Program Manager.

2. Open the Program Group window that contains the application icon that you want to start. You can open the Program Group window by choosing the W indow menu by pressing Alt-W , and then pressing the number associated with the Program Group name from the W indow menu.

3. Using the arrow keys, select the correct Program Item icon.

4. Press Enter to start the application or press Alt-F to choose the F ile menu, then press O to O pen the application.

To start an application using the mouse

1. Open the Program Manager.

2. Open the Program Group window that contains the
   application icon that you want to start. You can
   open the Program Group window by pointing to the
   open window and clicking the left mouse button. If
   the Program Group is in icon form, point to the
   Program Group icon and double-click the left
   mouse button.

3. Point to the Program Item icon with the mouse and
   double-click the left mouse button.

Notes

Rather than typing the name of the file that starts the
application at the DOS prompt, each application in
Windows is represented by a Program Item icon. An
icon is a graphic symbol that in some way represents the
type of application it will start. For example, the
Calculator accessory icon looks like a small calculator.

Windows applications have icons that are displayed in
the Program Manager. If the application is a DOS
application, however, you first must create a Program
Information File (PIF) and create a Program Item that
points to the PIF. The icon will represent a computer
screen with the word DOS on the screen, representing a
DOS application. You can change the icon of the DOS
application, however, to represent the type of application
that it is. One of the icons is a computer screen with a
telephone on the screen. This may represent a
communications program. By selecting the icon, you
easily can start the application.

Switching Applications

General

Purpose

Moves different applications into the foreground.

Procedures

To switch applications using the keyboard
Press Alt-Esc.

You move from application to application in a round-robin fashion. Even minimized applications (ones displayed as an icon) appear in the cycle. When a minimized application is the foreground application, the name appears highlighted under the icon. You can press **Alt-space bar** to choose the Control menu, and then choose to **R**estore or Ma**x**imize the icon.

To switch applications using the Task List

1. Press **Alt-Esc** or point to the Desktop and double-click the left mouse button. The Task List appears on-screen.

2. Use the arrow keys to select the application you want to make current. If you are using a mouse, point to the application and click the left mouse button.

3. Choose **S**witch To by pressing **Alt-S**, or by clicking the **Switch To** button with the left mouse button.

   If you are using a mouse, point to the application you want to switch to in the list and double-click the left mouse button.

   The application becomes active.

To switch applications using the mouse

Point to the application with the mouse and click the left mouse button. If other windows are in the way, you may have to move them. If the application you want to make current is displayed as an icon, point to the icon and double-click the left mouse button rather than performing Steps 2 and 3.

Note

When you have more than one application open, you must switch to the application that is in the foreground. You can switch between applications. You may use the mouse, keyboard, or call the Task List to switch applications. Normally, you will use the mouse or the keyboard. However, if you have several applications open, or if you seem to have lost the application that you want to switch to, use the Task List. The Task List lists all open windows from which you can choose.

Task List

General

Purpose

Switches among applications, closes applications, and arranges windows and icons.

Procedures

To switch to an application

1. Press **Alt-Esc**, or point to the Desktop and double-click the left mouse button.

   The Task List appears on-screen.

2. Use the arrow keys to select the application you want to make the current application.

   If you are using a mouse, point to the application and click the left mouse button.

3. Choose Switch To by pressing **Alt-S**, or by clicking the **Switch To** button with the left mouse button. (If you are using a mouse, you may point to the application to switch to in the list and double-click the left mouse button.) The application will become active.

To close an application

1. Press **Alt-Esc**, or point to the Desktop and double-click the left mouse button.

   The Task List appears on-screen.

2. Use the arrow keys to select the application you want to close.

   If you are using a mouse, point to the application and click the left mouse button.

3. Choose End Task by pressing **Alt-E**, or by clicking the **End Task** button with the left mouse button.

To arrange all open windows so that each window is in view, and of the same size (tiling)

1. Press **Alt-Esc**, or point to the Desktop and double-click the left mouse button.

The Task List appears on-screen.

2. Choose Tile by pressing **Alt-T**, or by clicking the Tile button with the left mouse button.

To arrange all open windows so that each window is stacked, and of the same size (cascading)

1. Press **Alt-Esc**, or point to the Desktop and double-click the left mouse button.

The Task List appears on-screen.

2. Choose Cascade by pressing **Alt-C**, or by clicking the Cascade button with the left mouse button.

To arrange all icons at the bottom of the screen

1. Press **Alt-Esc**, or point to the Desktop and double-click the left mouse button.

The Task List appears on-screen.

2. Choose Arrange Icons by pressing **Alt-A**, or by clicking the **Arrange Icons** button with the left mouse button.

Note

You can use the Task List to switch among active applications, whether they are windows or icons. If you switch to an icon, it not only is placed as the foreground application, but it is restored to a window. The Task List not only makes it easy to bring an application to the foreground, it will also enable you to manage tasks such as close them, arrange icons and windows to make tasks easier to find.

View a Directory

File Manager

Purpose

Opens a directory window to view the files contained in the directory.

Procedures

To view a directory

1. Start the File Manager accessory.

2. Choose the drive that contains the directory to view by pressing **Ctrl** and the letter associated with the drive. For example, to make drive C the current drive, press **Ctrl-C**.

   If you are using a mouse, point to the drive icon at the top of the Directory Tree window and press the left mouse button.

3. Open the directory by using the arrow keys to select the directory and press **Enter**, or choose the **F**ile menu and then choose **O**pen.

   If you are using a mouse, point to the directory to view and double-click the left mouse button. (If the directory is not displayed, then you may have the wrong drive, or the directory branch may be collapsed. Use the options from the **T**ree menu to expand directory branches.)

To close a directory

1. Select the directory window to close.

2. Choose the Control menu by pressing **Alt-space bar**, or by pointing to the Control menu with the mouse and clicking the left mouse button.

3. Choose **C**lose by pressing **C**, or by clicking **Close** with the left mouse button.

Note

The Directory Tree window displays all subdirectories for a disk drive. To view the files in the directory, you must open a directory window. Then you can select the files in the directory window to copy or delete.

Viewing Appointments

Calendar

Purpose

Displays an appointment.

Procedure

1. Start the Calendar accessory.

2. Open a Calendar file using the File Open command.

3. Choose the correct day for the appointment by pressing **Ctrl-PgUp** and **Ctrl-PgDn**, or by clicking the left and right scroll arrows with the mouse and then clicking the left mouse button.

4. When you have chosen the correct day, use the **up-** and **down-arrow** keys to scroll through the times.

   If you are using a mouse, point to the scroll box and press and hold the left mouse button. Drag the scroll box until the desired time comes in view.

Note

A calendar is only beneficial if you can view the appointments. The Calendar accessory makes it easy to view appointments, as you can switch from day to day, month to month to view appointments.

Viewing Cards

Cardfile

Purpose

Displays one of the cards in a cardfile.

Procedures

To view a card in card mode

1. Start the Cardfile accessory.

2. Open the cardfile using the File, Open command.

3. Choose the View menu by pressing Alt-V, or by clicking the View menu with the left mouse button.

   The current view appears with a check mark beside it in the View menu.

4. Choose Card by pressing C, or by clicking Card with the left mouse button.

To view cards in list mode

1. Start the Cardfile accessory.

2. Open the cardfile using the File, Open command.

3. Choose the View menu by pressing Alt-V, or by clicking the View menu with the left mouse button.

   The current view appears with a checkmark beside it in the View menu.

4. Choose List by pressing L, or by clicking List with the left mouse button.

Note

You can view a card in two ways. You can use Card view or List view. Although Card view displays one entire card at a time, List view only displays the index line of a card. However, in List view, all index lines are in alphabetic order. Rather than using Go To or Find to search for a card, you can List the index lines, scroll to the correct card, then switch to Card view to display the correct card.

Window Selection

General

(see *Switching Applications*).

Index